The Royal Road

150 Years of Enterprise

GREAT WESTERN RAILWAY COAT-OF-ARMS

The Royal Road

150 Years of Enterprise

by

Philip Rees OBE BSc (Eng) CE FICE
Chief Civil Engineer
BR (Western) 1975–83

Volume One of two volumes published
to mark the 150th anniversary of the
Great Western Railway
and its modern successor British Rail (Western)

ISBN 0 905466 68 3   © 1985

PUBLISHED BY BRITISH RAIL (WESTERN)
in association with
Avon-AngliA Publications & Services,
Annesley House, 21 Southside, Weston Super Mare, Avon. BS23 2QU

The Royal Road
150 Years of Enterprise

Contents

The illustrations on Page 2 cover three eras, that of the GWR broad gauge, the GWR heyday and the WR diesel-hydraulic period. The top scene shows the last broad gauge train in Sonning Cutting, the one below depicts a train emerging from the Severn Tunnel and the bottom scene is of the Cornish Riviera Express *at the Saltash end of the Royal Albert Bridge.*

Author's Preface

When the General Manger of the Western Region asked me if I would prepare a lecture to commemorate the 150th anniversary of the Great Western Railway I was doubtful about accepting the task but soon realised that, as one of the last chief officers to retire from the service of the Western Region who actually started his career on the Great Western Railway, it was appropriate that I should do so.

After some discussion it became clear that a short book based on the lecture would help to capture the occasion for posterity and what follows results from that discussion. After 45 years in the railway service, most of it spent in the civil engineering department of the Great Western Railway and the Western Region, and the last 8 years as Chief Civil Engineer, it will not be surprising that much of the book reflects a civil engineering outlook, but I hope also the outlook of a railwayman.

Most of the material I have used has been available from railway sources, but I am grateful to Mr O.S. Nock for his permission to use an extract from his book *The Great Western Railway in the Nineteenth Century*.

I am pleased to acknowledge the willing help of the Oxford Publishing Company in providing many of the illustrations for the book, and I am also indebted to the Great Western Railway Museum at Swindon for facilities to photograph the picture of Brunel's atmospheric system.

I must also record my appreciation of the assistance given by Major P. Olver and Mr A. Cooksey of the Department of Transport Railway Inspectorate in allowing me to inspect the official reports of railway accidents on the Great Western Railway and Western Region.

Finally, I must also express my gratitude for the willing help given to me by Mr R.W.N. Drummond, Regional Public Affairs Manager of the Western Region, by Mr G. Body of Avon-AngliA Publications and, not least, by my successor Mr D.L. Rowell, now designated Regional Civil Engineer, his former Administrative Assistant Mr N.E. Wade and his Survey Assistant Mr D. Faulkner and their most able staffs.

Chapter One

Beginnings

Among the events held to celebrate the Centenary of the Great Western Railway in 1935 was a banquet at which the principal guest was the Prince of Wales, who was later to become King Edward VIII. In his speech he graciously referred to the GWR's many associations with the Royal House and honoured the railway with the name 'The Royal Road' – hence the title of this book whose purpose 50 years later is to celebrate again, this time involving not only the Great Western Railway but also its successor, the Western Region of British Rail.

Others have already written, and no doubt will do so in the future, about the detailed history of the 'Western' and my aim is to remind ourselves of the significant events over this period of 150 years and, in bringing them to life again, rely not only on the recorded pages of history but also on personal memory spanning at least the last 50 of those years of enterprise and achievement.

Although over its history the Western has frequently been ahead of its sister railways in development, it was not the first main line railway to be built in this country. It was preceded by such well known lines as the Stockton & Darlington scheme of 1825 and the Liverpool & Manchester's line of 1830 although as early as 1824 a number of Bristol merchants and others were thinking seriously of the need to connect their city with London by this new means of transport. Indeed, the London and Bristol Rail-Road Company was formed with that famous road builder John Loudon Macadam as its engineer, but no Parliamentary powers to construct a railway were ever sought. It was not until the autumn of 1832 that further stirrings occurred and a meeting of local interests was held in Bristol on 21 January 1833 with one John Cave representing Bristol Corporation in the chair.

A sub-committee was subsequently formed to arrange for a preliminary survey and estimate and at this point they needed an engineer. A young man of 27, Isambard Kingdom Brunel, already well known in Bris-

tol in connection with the docks and Clifton Suspension Bridge projects, was appointed in March 1833 and promptly set about this task. He surveyed two principal routes, south and north of the Marlborough Downs respectively, and quickly decided to recommend the latter which followed the River Avon to Bath and then proceeded via Chippenham, Swindon, the Vale of the White Horse, Reading and the Thames Valley with a London terminus left unspecified for the time being.

The sub-committee prepared a detailed report which was presented to a public meeting in Bristol at which it was resolved that a company be formed to pursue the construction of a railway between Bristol and London. A body of directors for Bristol was appointed which, together with a similar body of directors for London, would form the General Board of Management for the company for securing subscriptions and obtaining an Act of Parliament. The first meeting of the Bristol and London Committees was held in London on 19 August 1833 and it was at this meeting that the title 'Great Western Railway' was adopted.

As sufficient shares had not been taken up to finance the whole route, the Board decided to apply to Parliament in 1834 for powers to construct only the lengths between Bristol and Bath and between London and Reading, the proposed London terminus being by the River Thames, near Vauxhall Bridge. A Bill was duly presented and passed its second reading in March 1834. In Committee the Bill occupied no less than 57 days during which opposition caused the company to move its proposed terminus to the Old Brompton Road. On passing to the Lords, however, the measure was defeated and the company had no alternative but to retreat and present a further Bill in 1835, this time for the whole line between London and Bristol, but with a significant change at the london end in that the line was shown to terminate at a junction with the London & Birmingham Railway near Wormwood Scrubs, the intention being to run Great Western trains into the

Early railway signalling as portrayed in the pages of the Illustrated London News

L&B's Euston terminus. Fortunately, this Bill had an easier passage through Parliament and received the Royal Assent on 31 August 1835.

The Great Western's Act contained 251 sections, some of which sound very odd today. For example, the company was not allowed to have any 'diversion, branch or station' within 3 miles of Eton College and was required to have 'a sufficient additional number of persons for the purpose of preventing or restricting all access to the said Railway by the scholars of Eton College'. Another interesting requirement was to pay compensation to Maidenhead Corporation for any annual decrease in their Thames Road bridge tolls for 6 years after the opening of the railway.

The negotiations with the London & Birmingham Railway soon fell through and in 1837 Parliamentary

powers were obtained for a terminus at Paddington.

During the period that the Bills had been passing through Parliament Brunel had been considering the question of the track gauge for the new railway, and it is significant that the Act of 1835 contained no reference to the gauge although the Bill of 1834 specified 4ft 8½ins (and it would be interesting to speculate upon the very different history of the Great Western that might have been written had that Bill become law). Brunel had come to the conclusion that the 4ft 8½ins gauge being used on other railways was too restrictive for his grand design of a line over which higher speeds with greater comfort were to be achieved and proposed a gauge of 7ft. Within a very short time of the Act being passed he raised this question with the directors and in October 1835 obtained their agreement.

The decision was a momentous one which was to affect the efficient performance of the locomotives, the speed of the trains and many other aspects of the new railway, but because of the 'break of gauge' problem at points where two railways of different gauges met the inconvenience and heavy costs of the transhipment of passengers and goods eventually spelled the doom of the broad gauge. Brunel and the Great Western were in a minority and the matter became one in which the Government took an interest by the appointment in 1845 of the Gauge Commission which, after considering the evidence of the parties, recommended not only that the gauge of all future railways should be 4ft 8½ins but also that lines already laid to the broad gauge should be converted to the narrow gauge.

The Commissioners' report was laid before Parliament in 1846 but no doubt because of the eternal question of 'who pays?' it did not insist on conversion of existing broad gauge lines and allowed others under construction, or shortly to be constructed, to be laid to this gauge where it made good sense operationally. In an even greater climb-down Parliament inserted a clause in the resulting Gauge Act of 1846 to the effect that the standard requirement to build future railways to the 4ft 8½ins gauge could be altered by specifying the gauge to be provided in the authorising Act of a particular line. And so most of the ammunition in the Gauge War was destroyed although, in practice, it spelled the eventual end of the broad gauge even if it was to be as much as 46 years later before it finally disappeared. Of this more presently.

Perhaps the most interesting relic of the broad gauge is Brunel's walking stick, for long the 'badge of office' of successive Chief Civil Engineers of the Great Western Railway and Western Region. It shows the inventiveness of Brunel since it unfolds in three hinged sections with gauge stops which measure exactly 7ft 0¼in, the recognised dimension of the broad gauge (although the reason for the extra ¼in remains in the area of speculation).

The author (left) opening out Brunel's walking stick with his successor Mr D.L. Rowell holding the handle and ferrule
British Rail

Chapter Two

Construction and Opening

Brunel had designed an excellent route with flat curves and, apart from three short lengths, with easy gradients not exceeding 1 in 660. Indeed, a total of 67 of the 118 miles were graded at 1 in 1320 or less. Two of the short lengths, together totalling only about 3¾ miles, were graded at 1 in 100 and were both west of Swindon – the first between Wootton Bassett and Dauntsey and the second through Box Tunnel. The summit of the line was at Swindon, a mere 270ft above Paddington and 292ft above the western terminus at Bristol. For such a route successive generations of railwaymen have ever been thankful to Brunel for his engineering skill which has enabled them to schedule speeds and loads far in excess of anything the great man himself envisaged.

Construction of the railway started from both the London and Bristol ends and the first contract was let before the end of 1835. This was for building the magnificent brick arch viaduct across the Brent valley at Hanwell, comprising eight spans of 70ft. It was named the 'Wharncliffe Viaduct' in honour of Lord Wharncliffe who, as chairman of the Lords' Committee considering the Great Western Railway Bill, had steered it successfully through the House.

The nature of the terrain dictated that most of the major civil engineering works including all the tunnels were west of Swindon, but in addition to the Wharncliffe Viaduct there were also some significant works to the east of Swindon. The best known of these is the brick arch bridge over the River Thames near Maidenhead. This comprised two main arches each of 128ft span with four side arches, one of 21ft and three of 28ft span, as flood openings on each side of the main spans. The rise of the main spans above springing level was only 24ft 3in and they were thus not only the flattest brick arches constructed to date but were widely predicted by critics to fall down as soon as the support of the centering was removed. In fact the western arch caused no problems at all but on easing the centering of the eastern arch the three lowest rings of brickwork

separated about ½in for 12ft on either side of the crown – and thus delighted the critics who were soon confounded, however, when the cause was established as the contractor's haste in easing the centering before the mortar had properly set. Brunel rightly required him to make good the defective work after which no further problems were experienced.

The approach to Reading had to contend with the hill at Sonning and Brunel had originally intended to tunnel under it. However, by building the line a little to the south a cutting 60ft deep and two miles long was substituted. This is the well known Sonning Cutting whose tree lined slopes have been much admired by

Sonning Cutting looking west and with an empty stone train on the Down Main line   *Author*

Maidenhead River Bridge showing the widening of the original arch (*Author*) and, below, the western portal of Box Tunnel *BR/OPC*

was quadrupled between 1890 and 1893. The Basildon and Moulsford bridges were widened by building new bridges of similar design alongside the originals, but Maidenhead bridge was widened to the original design on each side of the existing bridge. A different and ingenious scheme was adopted for widening Sonning Cutting. This was to raise the track level and at the same time to build retaining walls each side to cut back the toes of the cutting slopes, thus widening the formation sufficiently for the two additional tracks (which, of course, were narrow gauge by this time).

Contracts for construction of the original railway were approved and let independently by the London and Bristol Committees and it is significant that the latter commissioned designs which were often decidedly more elaborate than those for the London Committee. Indeed, the latter were recorded as complaining in early 1839 at what they considered to be unnecessary expenditure by their Bristol counterparts. At the Bristol end of the line examples of important original structures still in use today are the high retaining wall and short tunnels in Sydney Gardens just east of Bath, where the Kennet & Avon Canal was diverted to make room for the railway, and the tunnels between Bath and Bristol (although three of short length were opened out into cuttings many years ago). Another example is the River Avon bridge just east of Bristol whose elevations regrettably have been obscured on both sides by widening the line using steel bridges.

The original Temple Meads station, although no longer operational, is being preserved and has been leased for a peppercorn rent to the Brunel Engineering Centre Trust which has plans to restore the complex and use it as a museum. The building is a fine ornamental stone structure, and the roof of the train shed is magnificent.

The most important structure on the whole line, however, was undoubtedly the tunnel under Box Hill (between Chippenham and Bath) which is more than 1¾ miles long, 3,212 yards to be precise. It was started in 1836, and opened on 30 June 1841 along with the rest of the line between Chippenham and Bath. This was the last link which enabled to whole route to be opened throughout between Paddington and Bristol. As mentioned earlier, the tunnel was built on a gradient of 1 in

passengers but have also caused some anxiety to railway civil engineers from time to time because of the danger of trees being uprooted by gales. For this reason they are inspected regularly and any potentially dangerous trees felled before they can cause trouble.

Two further bridges over the River Thames between Reading and Didcot deserve mention; these are at Basildon and Moulsford respectively. Both are very similar and comprise four brick arches of 62ft span with Bath stone facings.

All of these structures have been carefully maintained by successive Chief Civil Engineers and their staffs and continue in use today but, of course, carrying vastly heavier and more frequent traffic than originally intended. They were, in fact, widened when the line

Contrasting views of the railway at Sydney Gardens Bath, left from a Bourne print and, below, a modern view with an Up HST. Both show the elegant design standards of the Bristol Committee of the Great Western Railway   *British Rail*

Another contrast, between the original Brunel train shed at Bristol with the classic roof spanning broad gauge tracks and, below, today's station with modern motive power and rolling stock   *Geoffrey Body*

100 falling towards Bath and that alone ensured that there would be few problems in draining away any water which entered the tunnel from the east end or, indeed, by seepage through the tunnel roof. For the greater part of the time that construction was in progress over 1,100 men and 100 horses were employed and it is salutory to note that the works claimed the lives of nearly 100 men during the period.

The eastern end of the tunnel passes through a thick bed of Bath stone and the structure in this area is unlined and, indeed, remains partly so to the present day although a brick lining was built over part of the length from the eastern mouth following some spalling of stone from the roof.

In those early days it was no doubt an eerie experience to travel through such a long tunnel by train in complete darkness. To allay public anxiety it was arranged to install lights through the tunnel but it seems that owing to the smoke and steam from the locomotives, which blocked out normal visibility, they were not very effective and were subsequently removed. The type of lamp used does not seem to have been recorded but they were no doubt rather primitive oil lamps.

The western portal of Box Tunnel is of particularly fine design and as the tunnel is absolutely straight it is possible to see from this point distant daylight at the eastern end, when the bore is clear of diesel fumes. There is an old legend that on Brunel's birthday, April 9th, an observer at the west end of the tunnel can see, through the tunnel, the sun as it rises over Box Hill. The well known railway author Mr O.S. Nock has checked the possibility of the legend's truth with the Superintendent of the National Almanac Office of the Royal Greenwich Observatory who told him that on April 9th the sun is definitely in a position to make this legend a fact. Perhaps the number of occasions when the early morning of April 9th has coincided with clear sky and a tunnel clear of steam or fumes is so rare that few people have actually seen the phenomenon in practice.

For his track Brunel departed from the accepted practice of the day of using short rails spanning stone blocks and adopted instead a 'bridge' rail laid on continuous longitudinal timbers on gravel ballast with transoms to maintain gauge every 15ft. In order to hold the track down he used wooden piles driven into the roadbed every 30ft and it was this which caused such severe problems immediately after the first section of line was opened.

This first section was from Paddington to Maidenhead and was opened on 4 June 1838, although the station called Maidenhead was in fact between Taplow and Maidenhead at the site of the skew bridge where the A4 trunk road passes under the line. Successive sections were opened in 1839 and 1840 but the railway had reached Challow from the London end before the first section from the Bristol end, as far as Bath, was opened on 31 August 1840. And, as we have already seen, progress from London had reached Chippenham before the final link in this mighty iron chain – between Chippenham and Bath – was eventually forged on 30 June 1841, almost six years after the Royal Assent to the 1835 Act; a remarkable achievement.

The opening of the line to Maidenhead soon provided serious problems for Brunel and for Gooch his young Locomotive Superintendent, for the riding of the carriages was far from satisfactory and the locomotives did not perform as well as necessary. Brunel soon realised that the use of piles for his track created solid spots every 30ft, while the length in between had settled slightly into the ballast and thus caused a switchback effect. All this created a furore among the opponents of the railway and the Board was forced to call in other eminent engineers to advise them. The resultant reports were unfavourable to both the broad gauge and the locomotives which, not unnaturally, caused some dissention among the directors. Chairman Charles Russell stood firm in his backing of Brunel and, as events turned out, a minor modification to the locomotive *North Star* carried out by Brunel and Gooch so improved its performance that the dissenters were largely silenced. Brunel was left to cut off the piles and pack the longitudinal timbers more effectively which improved the track and the quality of ride to acceptable levels.

This period must have been a most anxious time both for the directors and for Brunel, whose reputation was at stake. It is, however, an interesting early example of the results of working at the threshold of technology where experience is sometimes gained at the expense of failure.

Chapter Three

Extensions and Amalgamations

In the years when construction of the Great Western Railway was in progress there was increasing activity throughout the country in the promotion and building of more railways. Indeed, in 1845 and 1846 so many Bills for new lines were placed before Parliament that the period became known as the 'Railway Mania'.

The Great Western, London & South Western, the Grand Junction and the London & Birmingham Railways – the latter two being amalgamated into the London & North Western Railway in 1846 – all considered that there was territory into which they should expand with further lines to the exclusion of their rivals. Not unnaturally this led to many battles, legal and parliamentary, in which the LNWR particularly adopted any means, fair or foul, that appeared to enhance its purpose at the time.

The Great Western, naturally, championed its broad gauge and was anxious to extend it further into the West Country, in South Wales and, if possible, to head northwards to reach the River Mersey. In the two former areas the GWR was successful but, although its trains eventually reached Birkenhead, Parliament cut short its broad gauge ambitions at Wolverhampton. By this time, too, a number of lines were being laid with mixed broad and narrow gauge tracks by the expedient of using the rail nearest to the platform as common to both gauges with two other rails to suit the narrow and broad gauges respectively.

There were also cases where the Great Western, although not owning lines, made agreements with the owning companies to provide rolling stock and work the traffic on their behalf. Such was the arrangement between the Great Western and the Bristol & Exeter (another broad gauge Brunel railway) for eight years until 1849 when the B&E dismissed the Great Western and worked the line itself; an arrangement which stood for the next 27 years until 1876 when the two companies were formally amalgamated.

Two of the earliest companies with which the Great Western became associated were the Shrewsbury & Chester and the Shrewsbury & Birmingham, both being laid to the narrow gauge and opened between 1846 and 1849. Their independent history is largely one of opposition from the LNWR, always strong and sometimes of doubtful legality, and as a result they turned to the Great Western for help. This was at first by means of a working agreement and then, in 1854, by amalgamation which enabled the GWR's trains to reach the Mersey by use of the Shrewsbury & Chester's running powers between Chester and Birkenhead.

The Oxford, Worcester & Wolverhampton Railway, although independent, was strongly supported financially by the Great Western and its Act of 1845 specified that it should be of such gauge as would allow it to be worked continuously with the Great Western Railway. This was, of course, a rather roundabout way of saying that it must be broad gauge. However, the OW&W legal adviser who later became Deputy Chairman of the company, quickly came to dictate its policy and by his unscrupulous methods took every opportunity to battle with the Great Western. He flirted with their narrow gauge LNWR rival and clearly had no intention of laying the broad gauge throughout the line as the Act required. This saga lasted for six years until 1856 when a reconstituted Board brought in new directors who were much more friendly towards the Great Western. Agreement between the two companies was finally reached in 1858, but for the Great Western this was at the price of accepting only narrow gauge trains between Oxford and Wolverhampton.

In 1860 the OW&W amalgamated with two other narrow gauge companies, the Newport, Abergavenny & Hereford and the Worcester & Hereford, to form the West Midland Railway which itself was amalgamated with the Great Western in 1863.

Battles of a more friendly kind took place with the South Wales Railway. This railway from Grange Court, 7½ miles west of Gloucester, was to run via Chepstow,

Typical of the mixed gauge period, this view towards East Depot, Bristol shows where the original tunnel was converted to a cutting. Note that the siding connection is narrow gauge only
BR/OPC

Newport, Cardiff, Swansea and Carmarthen to Fishguard (later altered to Neyland, or New Milford as it became known) and to be broad gauge. It was leased to the Great Western who provided the locomotives and other rolling stock, together with the locomotive crews, but all other staff were employed by the South Wales Railway. The line was opened in stages between 1850 and 1856 and most of the arguments centred around the financial arrangements between the companies. They went on until 1863 when the two concerns were amalgamated.

The Great Western, retaining its own name throughout, thus became an even more powerful company controlling a large territory from London to Bristol, South Wales and the West Midlands and having close ties with the companies in Somerset and Devon which enabled through broad gauge trains to run from Paddington to Plymouth via Bristol and Exeter over the metals of three separate railway companies. Apart from

GREAT WESTERN RAILWAY 1863

Great Western Lines ━━━━━━
Other Lines ···········

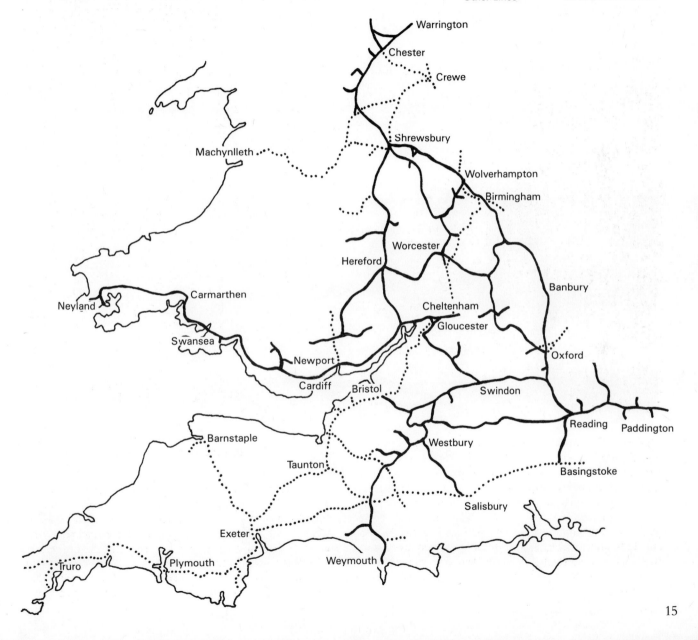

15

the Great Western these were the Bristol & Exeter and the South Devon Railway, a grouping known as 'the Associated Companies'.

Beyond Plymouth the broad gauge Cornwall Railway, supported by the Associated Companies, opened as far as Truro in 1859 and to Falmouth in 1863. The West Cornwall Railway, from Truro to Penzance, was laid to the narrow gauge but was converted to mixed gauge to allow the through running of passenger trains from Paddington to Penzance from 1 March 1867.

The Great Western map thus changed dramatically between 1841 and 1863 by which time the company had also become a dual gauge railway which retained the broad gauge in part of the original main line to Bristol and also in South Wales but had significant mileages of mixed and narrow gauge track, the latter being mostly in the Midlands and North.

The inconvenience of working separate broad and narrow gauge trains must have been considerable, in spite of the use of mixed gauge track to obviate the need to tranship goods and passengers. But another 29 years were to pass before the broad gauge finally disappeared.

A scene on the coastal section of the former South Devon Railway near Teignmouth. This is the last broad gauge train west and the permanent way transoms have been cut ready for conversion *BR/OPC*

Chapter Four

Great Western Personalities

Those who successfully shape the fortunes of large organisations do so usually because they are good managers of people for it is well motivated people who can make an organisation work. Such were many of the first Great Western officers, but there were four who were outstanding and we do well to pause awhile to look at them and their contributions to the greatness of the Western.

Apart from Brunel, there were Daniel Gooch the Locomotive Superintendent who became chairman from 1865 to 1889, Charles Saunders, Secretary and General Superintendent, and Charles Russell, Chairman from 1839 to 1855.

Isambard Kingdom Brunel, to quote his full name, was a brilliant engineer whose work extended beyond railways to docks and ships. Indeed, many of his structures bear the marks of an architect as well as a civil engineer. He was kindly and considerate but a strict disciplinarian and is recorded as warning severely a young member of his staff who did not measure up to his requirements. He was a man who led by example and drove himself hard in the pursuit of his objectives. His output of work was phenomenal. Indeed, it was probably this which contributed to his death in 1859 at the early age of 53.

Brunel had his failures as well as his successes and his greatest failure was probably the use of the atmospheric system of propulsion on the South Devon Railway between Exeter and Newton Abbot. This required the laying between the rails of a 15in diameter pipe in which was a piston, connected to a trolley attached to the train. Lineside pumping stations were used to exhaust the air from the pipe and thus draw the piston along. Although tried with greater success in South London and in Ireland, the punishing seaside atmosphere of the South Devon line caused corrosion of the continuous valve and other problems which defied solution at reasonable cost. The system was therefore abandoned after twelve months trial and ordinary locomotives substituted.

The last Brunel viaduct, Collegewood on the Falmouth branch, in the process of being replaced by a new brick-arched viaduct with masonry piers   *BR/OPC*

One of the unusual structures for which Brunel is remembered is the timber viaduct. These carried the railway over rivers and valleys in Devon and Cornwall and, indeed, there were 34 of them between Plymouth and Truro. All have now been replaced, mainly by brick and masonry arched viaducts, but it was as recently as 1934 that the last of the timber structures was demolished.

Brunel's last and greatest achievement was undoubtedly the Royal Albert Bridge at Saltash which carried a single line of the Cornwall Railway across the River Tamar. It comprised two main spans each of 455ft and seventeen approach spans varying from 69ft 6ins to 93ft. The unusual design of the main spans, which are still in use today, mark the bridge out as probably the only example of its kind in the world. The two approach spans at the Saltash end were subsequently reconstructed and widened in 1909 to allow the single to double line junction to be located on the bridge and in

1928 the remaining 15 approach spans were reconstructed and, of course, continue in use. The whole bridge has been maintained carefully by successive generations of Western civil engineers, carrying out repairs when needed and also, in recent years, strengthening to enable heavier axle loads to pass over it. Although not quite in the category of the 'continuous painting' of the Forth Bridge, the Royal Albert Bridge is nonetheless partially repainted each year in accordance with a 6-year programme so that the whole bridge is completely repainted to this cycle.

The Royal Albert Bridge was formally opened by HRH the Prince Consort, who gave his name to it, in May 1859 but unfortunately Brunel's failing health prevented his being present to enjoy the triumphant fulfilment of his plans. He was subsequently to ride over the bridge on a specially prepared truck but he died only a few months later in September 1859.

Brunel is remembered by a statue at Paddington station, generously given by the Bristol & West Building Society who also have another statue outside their Bristol headquarters offices. A third statue of Brunel is in the Brunel Shopping Centre at Swindon.

As a reminder of their heritage to present day Chief Civil Engineers a bust of Brunel stands on the shelf in the CCE's private office. Long may it remain there as an inspiration to greatness.

Originally Brunel had been solely responsible for locomotives and carriages as well as for the purely civil engineering side of the new railway, but as early as 1837 he saw the need for a specialist engineer to look after this important part of the undertaking. The Board soon authorised him to take on someone for these duties and later that year he engaged a young man, not yet 21 years old. His name was Daniel Gooch, and thus started an association with the Great Western Railway which was to have a profound effect upon its fortunes over many years.

The first Great Western engines were not of Gooch's design and, as mentioned earlier, were not performing satisfactorily. Part of the responsibility for this lay with Brunel who specified some of the principal requirements, including a maximum weight, and partly with the contractors who built them. Gooch spent a great deal of his time in his early years of service getting the best out of a rather motley bunch of machines and only those built by Robert Stephenson & Co of Newcastle were generally reliable enough to be used extensively in service. In 1839 the Board agreed that future engines should be designed by Gooch who issued a complete specification of his requirements to the contractors. Indeed, to ensure that many parts were interchangeable he provided the contractors with templates. This was the first occasion on which a measure of standardisation was achieved and was a fore-runner of the much greater standardisation achieved in Great Western locomotive practice in later years. In passing it may be noted that the first locomotive to be built at Swindon Works was turned out in 1846 and thereafter the majority were built at GWR workshops rather than by contractors as hitherto.

Gooch was a man who liked to see things for himself and often visited the locomotive builders' works to ensure that his requirements were being met and that the Great Western was getting what it was paying for. He also drove his locomotives, for what better way than

Gooch's diaries recorded '*North Star* and the six (engines) from Vulcan were the only ones I could at all depend upon'
BR/OPC

19

that to assess their ability to achieve the desired performance in service. Gooch tells the story of one occasion when he was acting as pilotman through Box Tunnel (then only a single line) on the locomotive of the last Up train of the day and in the distance he thought he could distinguish some green lights. At that period all Great Western engines carried green headlamps and he quickly realised that there was a train approaching on the same track. Gooch immediately reversed his train and ran back out of the tunnel and so avoided a terrible accident. In those days safety arrangements were rather primitive by present standards.

In 1864 Gooch decided to resign in order to take up an opportunity of laying the first Atlantic cable, but in this he was unsuccessful at the first attempt. A year later and before making a further attempt he was invited to join the Great Western Railway Board and become its Chairman. This invitation he accepted and occupied the Chair for 24 years from 1865 until his death in 1889.

Soon after becoming chairman Gooch organised another attempt at laying an Atlantic cable, using Brunel's ship *Great Eastern*, and this time he succeeded. He sent the first telegram from America to Ireland in 1865 and for this great achievement he was recognised

by the Queen in the award of a baronetcy.

As chairman Sir Daniel had to steer the Great Western through a period of severe financial difficulty but, so successful was he in doing so, that the company's dividend, which had fallen to 1⅜% in 1868, was raised to 6¼% in 1873 and after 1880 never fell below 5% during his term of office. In recognition of his achievement the shareholders gave Gooch a spontaneous gift of 5,000 guineas in 1872. His death in 1889 at the age of 73 robbed the Great Western of its most outstanding servant.

Charles Saunders entered the company's service in 1833 at the age of 37 as Secretary to the London Committee and was tireless in enlisting support and securing subscriptions for the shares of the company which was so necessary before a Bill could be laid before Parliament. So much were his efforts appreciated that at the Board Meeting in October 1835, the first after the passing of the Great Western Railway Act, the proprietors requested the directors to present him with a gratuity in addition to his salary.

Saunders was a man of great integrity and (in contrast to certain officers of other railway companies) he was a man of his word who, although he did not enter into agreements lightly or without tough negotiation, rightly regarded them as binding and acted accordingly. In 1840 he was promoted to be Secretary and General Superintendent of the Line and thus became the Board's first chief executive officer. The Great Western, unlike most other railway companies, did not have a general manager, that function being carried out by the Board, and Saunders' role was to ensure that his Board's policies were carried out and to assist the heads of departments to exercise their management. These heads of department, however, reported direct to the Board.

Saunders always insisted on courtesy in dealing with the public as well as harmonious working amongst the officers and staff of the various departments. While the former requirement, after too many lapses, is now being pursued again with vigour, the latter has carried through to the present day. While naturally there are sometimes differences of view amongst officers in the Board Room, this does not in any way affect the underlying harmony which has long been a hallmark of Western management.

Brunel's atmospheric system on the South Devon Railway.
From a drawing in the *Great Western Railway Museum,
Swindon*

Over the years Charles Saunders had been involved in all the battles with rival companies (some of whom, regretably, could not be relied upon to honour agreements made with the Great Western), and also with many Parliamentary Committees. He was a most devoted servant but unfortunately, in 1862 at the age of 66, his health deteriorated and he retired in September 1863. In November of that year Queen Victoria presented him with a handsome silver centrepiece – in her words 'As a mark of Her Majesty's approval of your services in attendance on Her Majesty on every occasion for very many years past on which she has travelled on the Great Western Railway'. Unfortunately, even the release from heavy responsibility in retirement was insufficient to restore Saunders' health and he died in September 1864.

Charles Russell was MP for Reading and was chairman of the Committee of the House of Commons which considered the Great Western Bills of both 1834 and 1835. It was his support which assured success for the Bill which became the Great Western Act of 1835. Not long after this he was elected a director of the company and became chairman in 1839, an office which he held with distinction until 1855.

Russell was not only a staunch supporter of Brunel, Saunders and the broad gauge but was also well liked and respected by the staff, with whom he came in contact much more than most present day company chairmen. He presided over the Great Western's affairs at a time of recession but the Great Exhibition of 1851 brought extra traffic which enabled a dividend ½% higher than the previous year's at 4½% to be distributed, and also enabled gratuities to be given to the staff who had worked hard to carry the additional traffic.

Early in 1852 the staff collected a sum of £420 to be used to obtain a full length portrait of Russell which was to be placed in the Board Room at Paddington as a testimonial 'of their grateful esteem for the high principles of honour, impartiality and undeviating kindness which he has ever displayed towards them.' The eminent painter chosen was Francis Grant, RA.

The staff in those days were occasionally required to appear in the Board Room before the directors at inquiries, either as culprit or witness, and such visits became known amongst them as 'going to see the picture'!

In 1855, in his 70th year, increasing ill-health caused Russell to resign and it is sad to record that his illness affected his brain and he died by his own hand in 1856. He had been the first of a select band of great chairmen of the Great Western.

It is an interesting coincidence that the ages of these four Great Western stalwarts were all separated by ten years – Russell, Saunders, Brunel and Gooch in that descending order.

Charles Russell

Chapter Five

The End of the Broad Gauge

By 1866 it had become apparent to a rather reluctant Great Western Board that the problems caused by the transhipment of traffic at stations where the broad and narrow gauge met, then about twenty in number, were causing increasingly loud complaints from the commercial world and probably loss of revenue as well. The traders of South Wales were the most vocal and they approached the Board with a firm request that the whole of their territory should be converted to the narrow gauge.

At this time the Great Western comprised about 600 route miles of broad gauge, 230 of mixed gauge and 420 of narrow gauge, so that the task was a formidable one and likely to be expensive. The company also had financial problems at the same time and was unlikely to obtain any Government assistance to ease the burden of carrying out the work. The result in 1866 was the inevitable one of postponement until better times prevailed.

However it was only two years later that a modest start was made in an unusual way. The independent Pembroke & Tenby Railway, a narrow gauge concern, had recently extended its line to Whitland on the South Wales main line and set its eyes further afield towards the narrow gauge of the London & North Western Railway at Llandovery and thus to through traffic from the north. The missing narrow gauge link was between Whitland and Carmarthen, there being already a narrow gauge line from Carmarthen to Llandeilo and onward to Llandovery.

Hitherto the Great Western had rejected the Pembroke company's requests to mix the gauge between Whitland and Carmarthen and the lever which opened the way to Carmarthen was a P&T Bill for its own line between these points. The Great Western responded by reaching an agreement to convert its Up line between Whitland and Carmarthen Bridge to the narrow gauge for use as a single line by P&T trains while retaining the Down line as a broad gauge single line for its own

trains, which at that time were not numerous and well capable of being worked over one line. The P&T company contributed £20,000 to the cost of this work and also built, at its own cost, a new West curve from Carmarthen Bridge to Carmarthen Town station.

Some other conversions were carried out on a few minor lines during the ensuing 3–4 years but it was not until 1871 that the Great Western finally 'grasped the nettle' and came forward with a major scheme to convert the whole of its South Wales lines to the narrow gauge together with the line between Swindon and Gloucester, the line between Gloucester and Grange Court having been converted already to mixed gauge as part of the Gloucester to Hereford scheme. To complete the South Wales project, a third rail for the narrow gauge was to be added between Didcot and Swindon, thus allowing narrow gauge trains to run throughout from Paddington to South Wales.

Wisely, such a major project – which involved converting 424 miles of running lines, apart from sidings – was planned to be carried out during the summer and a start on 1 May 1872 was arranged. Prior to this, of course, there was detailed planning between the Engineering and Traffic officers and it was considered that a whole month would be required for the work. It was clearly impossible to shut the railway for such a lengthy period and, as the main line was double, it was decided to convert one line at a time while running over the other a limited train service which could be accommodated on a single line with passing loops at a number of main stations.

The local permanent way staff were supplemented by large numbers of men drafted in from other parts of the system and were organised into gangs of ten men with an Inspector supervising two gangs. Work commenced as planned at daybreak on 1 May and the Up line was completed ready for narrow gauge trains to run on 12 May. Work then started on the Down line which was completed on 22 May and normal double line working

Gauge conversion at Plymouth (Millbay) in May 1892. The work, which includes a new profile for the edge of one platform, seems to be going well *BR/OPC*

was resumed on the following day. Work on the Swindon – Gloucester line was then immediately started, one line at a time as in South Wales, and this was completed on 28 May. Most of the branches and sidings were converted to narrow gauge during the same month.

Apart from about 40 miles of cross-sleepered track, the whole of the track was formed of bridge rail on longitudinal timbers, and the fact that the entire work was carried out to schedule reflected not only the careful planning but also the maximum possible preparatory work carried out under traffic and before taking possession of the line.

Redundant broad gauge rolling stock stored at Swindon prior to breaking up. A poignant sight, with 4, 5 and 8-compartment coaches plus vans and trucks   *BR/OPC*

Following the conversion of one or two minor lines, 1873 saw the Great Western with no broad gauge remaining north of the Paddington – Bristol main line, apart from the Henley and Faringdon branches (which were converted in 1876 and 1878 respectively). Equally,

there was no narrow gauge west of the Reading to Basingstoke line.

The next significant area to be converted was, therefore, south of the Bristol main line comprising mainly the route from Thingley Junction, near Chippenham, and Bathampton to Westbury, Salisbury and Dorchester, together with associated branches. By the end of 1876 the Great Western had become wholly a mixed and narrow gauge railway except for the Faringdon branch and the broad gauge was required only to serve the South Devon and Cornwall Railways with through trains. It is surprising, therefore, that another seventeen years were to pass before it finally disappeared and only then, apparently, following a prod from the Cornwall Railway directors in 1885, the Bristol & Exeter Railway by then being already a mixed gauge line, having amalgamated with the Great Western in 1876. Before anything positive was done on the ground, the Cornwall Railway was also amalgamated with the Great Western – this in 1889.

With such long notice, the Great Western had designed and built most of its new rolling stock required for the broad gauge as suitable for conversion to the narrow gauge and thus the outlay was minimised when the time for the conversion of gauge finally arrived.

The GWR directors now called for a full report from the general manager on the scale and cost of the conversion remaining, including savings which would accrue from it. He reported that there remained 171 route miles of solely broad gauge running line, only 42 of which were double, making a total of 213 track miles to be converted at an estimated cost of £78,227 which included some bridge strengthening, especially in Cornwall. Against this could be set the net value of the third rail and its timbers on those lines which still had the mixed gauge, which amounted to £107,782, and also a figure of £5,531 for the traffic savings from the avoidance of transhipment and shunting associated with the broad gauge. There was thus a good financial case for doing the work and it was decided that it should be carried out in May 1892 during only one weekend, a task requiring the most careful preparation and planning.

The last broad gauge train to leave Paddington for Penzance was the 10.15am on Friday 20 May 1892 which, with several additional stops, was timed to reach its destination at 8.20pm and to return its empty coaches from Penzance to Swindon at 9.10pm as the last broad gauge train from Penzance, all other broad gauge rolling stock, both passenger and goods, having been worked away beforehand. Narrow gauge stock to replace it was worked down from Exeter to Plymouth via the L&SWR route on the same day in readiness for starting

up the service again on Monday 23 May.

As with the South Wales operation in 1872 large numbers of men were drafted into the area from all over the system, in this case some 3,400 to add to the 1,300 from the Plymouth Engineering Division.

As soon as the 9.10pm train from Penzance had passed, the line was handed over to the engineers who worked long shifts on the Saturday and Sunday and in some cases completed their work ahead of schedule. In no case was the resumption of traffic delayed and the Sunday night mail train from Paddington, which reached Plymouth from Exeter by the London & South Western route, was timed to leave there for Penzance at 4.40am on the Monday and duly did so.

It is interesting to note that during the period of the engineers' occupation, mails for Cornwall were transferred from the train at Plymouth to Millbay Docks where one of the company's Channel Islands steamers was waiting convey them, and also passengers including day trippers, to Fowey and Falmouth. A similar arrangement operated in the reverse direction.

The main ingredient for success in such a major task was then, as now, careful planning, the maximum of preparatory work carried out before the occupation and good supervision of staff on the day. On this occasion the hope of every engineer responsible for such major tasks – good weather – was realised and must have assisted considerably in the triumph which was achieved and earned great credit for all those who were engaged in it.

Perhaps one of the most imaginative pieces of preparatory work was in connection with the conversion over the Royal Albert Bridge at Saltash. Here, on a number of previous weekends, a narrow gauge track had been laid between the rails of the broad gauge track so that on the final conversion day all that was needed was to slew the track on either side of the bridge to meet the new metals.

So the 'break of gauge' problem was finally solved although British Rail does still have one 'break of gauge' station remaining at Aberystwyth now, sadly, no longer part of the Western Region. From a separate platform at the main station the 1ft 11½in gauge trains of the Vale of Rheidol line run to Devil's Bridge carrying thousands of passengers in the summer months.

Chapter Six

New Lines and Shorter Journeys

Not without some justification, the Great Western Railway towards the end of the 19th century was sometimes described as the 'Great Way Round' referring, of course, to its rather less than direct routes from London to Devon and Cornwall via Bristol, to South Wales via Gloucester, to Birmingham via Oxford and also between Birmingham and Bristol. In the latter case the Midland Railway already had a direct route via Gloucester over which the Great Western had running powers between Standish Junction and Yate, north of Bristol.

It was not only distance which gave this stigma to the Great Western for the chief officer in charge of operating at the time was, perhaps, one of the most unprogressive officers ever employed by the company and had a wholesale dislike of average speeds higher than 40mph. On his retirement in 1888 the way was open for a considerable speeding up of trains, even on the rather roundabout routes, until new lines could overcome the problem of distance.

However, the first rumblings for a shorter route to South Wales came much earlier in a suggestion for a tunnel under the River Severn, in 1865. The existing route from Paddington was via Swindon and Gloucester, while access from Bristol to South Wales was via branch lines connecting with a ferry between New Passage near Pilning and Portskewett on the Welsh side.

It was not until 1872, however, that the Great Western obtained an Act for a line under the Severn between Pilning on the Gloucestershire side of the river and Rogiet (now called Severn Tunnel Junction) on the Welsh side. The tunnel, about 4½ miles long, was to be sited at a point where the river is 2¼ miles wide and was originally designed to have gradients of 1 in 100 on each side with a short level section in the middle. Surface water entering the tunnel from either end was to be pumped out from a shaft at Sudbrook on the Welsh bank of the river.

Work was started in 1873 at Sudbrook, using direct labour, on a shaft and pilot tunnel to ascertain the nature of the ground through which the main bore was to be driven. Progress was steady, mainly through sandstone. By the middle of 1879 shafts had been sunk on both sides of the river, most being on the Welsh side since much more of the tunnel on this side was under land than on the English side. At that time, too, the headings from each side came within 130 yards of each other.

Then, on 16 October 1879, the first of several serious setbacks hit the project. Water from what became known as the Great Spring, lying under land on the Welsh slope of the tunnel, burst into the workings at such a rate that the workforce had quickly to evacuate the headings and in a very short time the shaft at Sudbrook was flooded to a depth of 150 feet. Work came to a standstill and, apart from pumping, remained so for more than a year.

After seven years work and considerable expenditure on the project the Great Western directors were in no mood to abandon it and they asked Sir John Hawkshaw, previously their consulting engineer, to take direct charge of the work. This he agreed to do provided he could select a contractor in whom he had confidence to complete all the works, and to this the directors agreed.

Hawkshaw decided to deepen the tunnel by 15ft which, although maintaining the gradient on the English side at 1 in 100, required that on the Welsh side to be increased to 1 in 90. Additional pumping equipment was provided, headwalls were erected in the tunnel to cut off the Great Spring temporarily and work resumed in December 1880; but it was only a few months afterwards, in the following April, that another setback occurred – this time on the English slope.

The profile of the bed of the River Severn features a deep channel on the Welsh side known as 'The Shoots' and shallow rocks, visible at low tide, on the English side. It was from a fissure in these rocks that water from the river now found its way in considerable quantities into the tunnel, fortunately not yet completed under the river so that the flooding was confined to the English side. The fissure in the rocks was located and plugged with clay and concrete and, after pumping out the tunnel, work was restarted. It progressed steadily for over two years, with the two headings under the river meeting in September 1881 and the tunnel being enlarged to its full profile with a brick lining. Another heading was being excavated from the original shaft at Sudbrook in order to lead the water from the Great Spring to the pumps clear of the tunnel when, in October 1883, it suddenly burst through with even greater force than in 1879 and soon flooded the workings again, including on this occasion the under-river part of the tunnel.

To add to this problem a week later a tidal wave in the Severn flooded low-lying land on the Welsh side of the river and water found its way into one of the shafts to the west of the Great spring and flooded the tunnel to within 8ft of the soffit of the arch. About eighty men were trapped on staging used by the bricklayers building the tunnel lining and they were only rescued by the lowering of a small boat end on down the shaft and using it to ferry them back to the shaft and safety.

Fortunately these were the last of the major incidents and when the water was pumped out work proceeded normally again and the waters of the Great Spring were led through a small, specially-constructed tunnel alongside the railway to the main pumping shaft. It was fitting that in October 1884 Sir Daniel Gooch should be the first to pass through the breakthrough hole between headings which signalled the completion throughout of a way under the river. The whole tunnel was finally completed and the track laid for a celebration train carrying the directors and their guests on 5 September 1885. There remained some work to complete on the approach cuttings and on the ventilation equipment, comprising a massive fan at Sudbrook, and this delayed the opening for passenger trains until December 1886.

After it was brought into full use the tunnel rarely became clear of the steam and smoke of the considerable number of trains which were routed through it, and the damp atmosphere caused corrosion of the rails to such an extent that their life was as little as three years in some parts of the tunnel. While this problem was improved with diesel traction, the atmosphere remains damp and the rails are now renewed every six years to ensure that fractures do not occur. The present track is, of course, entirely continuous welded rail on concrete sleepers.

The author has inspected the tunnel throughout on foot on several occasions and apart from a few areas of minor leakage in the brickwork it remains in very good condition. The brickwork in the shafts and the small tunnel conveying the water of the Great Spring is in remarkably fine condition for a structure now almost 100 years old.

The steam operated Cornish beam engines working the pumps were replaced in 1961 by modern electric submersible pumps which every day remove up to 30 million gallons of water from the tunnel, most of which is conveyed away and sold to local industry.

The Severn Tunnel enabled trains between London and South Wales to travel via Bath and reduced their journey by 15 miles compared with the Gloucester route. However, the Bath route was becoming so congested that some relief became essential by the turn of the century and the alternatives of quadrupling this route or building an entirely new line by a route shortening the distance to South Wales still further were considered. Wisely the directors chose the latter course and so the route from Wootton Bassett, 6 miles west of Swindon, to Patchway via Badminton, a distance of 30 miles, was started in 1897. The ruling gradient was 1 in 300 which represented a considerable improvement on the two gradients of 1 in 100 on the Bath route, but this achievement involved fairly heavy earthworks, mostly in clay, and two tunnels. The longest, Sodbury Tunnel, was just over 2½ miles long and on a completely straight alignment. The line was opened in 1903 and not only reduced the distance to South Wales by a further 11 miles but, perhaps more importantly, reduced the journey time by 25 minutes.

The shortening of the route from London to Devon and Cornwall was achieved by building three new lines to connect with existing lines which were themselves doubled and brought up to main line standards where necessary. One of the new routes was in Wiltshire, between Patney and Westbury, and the other two were in Somerset, between Castle Cary and Langport and between Athelney and Cogload Junction, 5 miles east of Taunton. The Patney to Westbury line was opened in

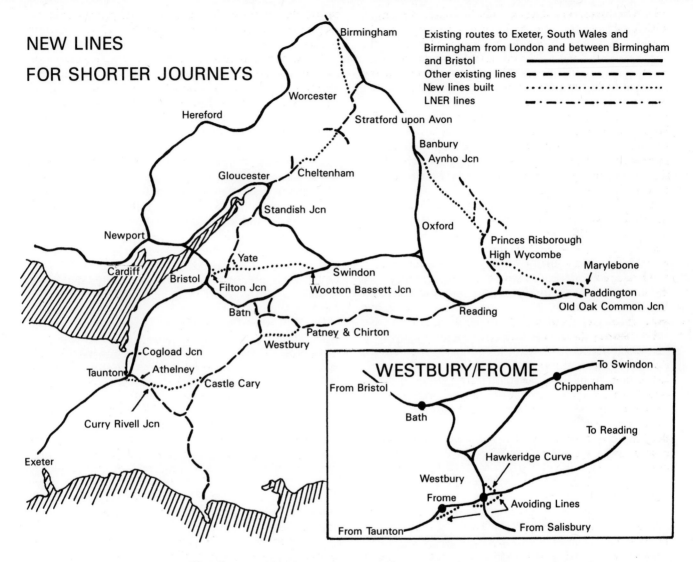

NEW LINES
FOR SHORTER JOURNEYS

Existing routes to Exeter, South Wales and Birmingham from London and between Birmingham and Bristol ——————
Other existing lines — — — —
New lines built ·················
LNER lines —·—·—·—

Birmingham
Worcester
Hereford
Stratford upon Avon
Banbury
Aynho Jcn
Gloucester
Cheltenham
Standish Jcn
Oxford
Princes Risborough
High Wycombe
Marylebone
Newport
Cardiff
Yate
Bristol
Swindon
Filton Jcn
Wootton Bassett Jcn
Reading
Paddington
Old Oak Common Jcn
Batn
Patney & Chirton
Westbury
Cogload Jcn
Taunton
Athelney
Castle Cary
Curry Rivell Jcn
Exeter

WESTBURY/FROME

From Bristol
To Swindon
Bath
Chippenham
To Reading
Hawkeridge Curve
Westbury
Frome
Avoiding Lines
From Taunton
From Salisbury

1900 and benefited passengers from Paddington to Yeovil, Dorchester and Weymouth by reducing their journey by 14 miles but, of course, had no effect as yet on Devon and Cornwall passengers. Indeed, it was not until 1906 that the remaining two legs of the route were completed and from this date the whole route to Taunton and beyond was shortened by 20 miles.

The London to Birmingham route was shortened by building two new cut off lines, both of them in conjunction with the Great Central Railway which was extending its system to London. The new lines were from Old Oak Common, 3 miles from Paddington, to High Wycombe, from which point the existing line to Princes Risborough was improved and doubled, and from Princes Risborough to Aynho Junction 5 miles south of Banbury. The Great Central built a new line from

29

Neasden to Northolt Junction (with a burrowing junction at the latter point) and from Northolt right through to Ashendon Junction the line became joint between the two companies. At Ashendon Junction the Great Central diverged to its main line at Grendon Underwood Junction while the Great Western built its own line onwards to Aynho Junction.

Two interesting features of this route are worth recording. In improving the High Wycombe to Princes Risborough section, hitherto a single line branch, the existing single line between Saunderton and Princes Risborough with a gradient of 1 in 88 falling to Princes Risborough was retained as the Down line, while the Up line was built as a new line nearby but with a much flatter gradient of 1 in 167. The other interesting feature is that both Ashendon and Aynho Junction were constructed as flying junctions, although it is very doubtful whether the traffic justified the extra expenditure.

The section of route from Old Oak Common to Ashendon Junction was opened in 1905 but the Great Western extension to Aynho Junction was not opened until 1910, making this the last of the new 'cut-offs'. While shortening the Great Western route to Birmingham by 18 miles it also made it 2 miles shorter than the competing L&NWR route from Euston via Rugby.

At the turn of the century the Great Western routes between Birmingham and Bristol were either via Hereford and the Severn Tunnel or via Oxford and Swindon, neither of which carried through trains. The Midland Railway route via Cheltenham was 89 miles long and quite direct so that there was little the Great Western could do to equal it. However, in order to compete for the valuable West of England traffic the GWR had to do the next best and this was achieved by building two new lines, respectively from Tyseley, about 4 miles south of Birmingham Snow Hill, to join the Stratford-on-Avon branch 3½ miles north of that town, and from Honeybourne to Cheltenham. The Great Western southbound trains then took the avoiding line at Gloucester and joined the Midland line at Standish Junction, having running powers over it as far as Yate whence a new short connecting line was built to join the new South Wales Direct line at Westerleigh Junction. The distance from Birmingham to Bristol by this route was 99 miles and it was opened throughout in 1908.

Journey times as shown in the 1912 Bradshaw were around 2 hours by the Midland route with stops at Cheltenham, Gloucester and Mangotsfield and about 2 hours 20 minutes by the Great Western route with stops at Stratford-on-Avon, Cheltenham and Bristol Stapleton Road.

By 1910, therefore, the Great Western had changed from being a slow and unpopular railway to being the most progressive in the country whose timetables compared well for speed and frequency with those of all the other main line companies.

Cogload Junction, east of Taunton, showing the flyover
BR/OPC

Chapter Seven

World War I and the 1923 Amalgamation

The first World War called for supreme efforts, not only from those in the armed services but also from the industries which provided their essential back-up. The Great Western Railway was thus in the front line on the Home Front in moving thousands of train loads of troops, munitions and equipment and it did so with great credit.

In August 1914 the Government took over the railways, with day-to-day control in the hands of a Railway Executive Committee, chaired by the President of the Board of Trade and with the general managers of the principal railway companies as its members. Financial compensation to the companies was agreed based on the net receipts for the year 1913 but, in the event, the Government had the best of the deal from the Great Western whose wartime traffic increased by no less than 23%, compared with only 2–3% for some other major companies.

It is surprising that, in spite of the increased war traffic, the passenger timetable was not thinned out and people travelled by train as much as previously. There was considerable difficulty in maintaining services, however, in view of the number of staff enlisted into the Armed Forces; over 25,000 men, or about one third of the 1914 workforce. Wherever possible they were replaced by women, youths and retired staff re-employed, but there remained many problems in coping with the increased traffic and by 1916 it became clear that there would have to be a reduction in passenger services if the increasing demands of the Forces were to be met. So, from 1 January 1917, many express trains were taken off and additional stops put into others. Some lightly used stations and branch lines were temporarily closed to ease the problem of staffing and the provision of locomotives so badly needed for the war traffic.

Swindon Works was used to build ambulance trains and also manufacture guns and ammunition in large quantities. Many new military depots were built, including a very large Ordnance Depot at Didcot, all of which required many miles of sidings and connections to the main line. The army commander in France was also demanding large quantities of track, locomotives and wagons for military railways and depots and the Great Western provided 95 locomotives, over 6,000 wagons and 49 miles of track (much of it taken up from the temporarily closed branches) towards his requirements. Inevitably maintenance at home suffered, track and structures received less than their normal attention and renewals were deferred.

Although fares had increased by 50% in January 1917, this was the first increase during the war and as yet there was no increase in freight rates, although the trade unions had negotiated wage increases and an eight hour day. The result was an increase in the wage bill from about £6 million in 1914 to over £14 million in 1919. Together with the heavy increase in the cost of coal and materials this had doubled the working expenses of the Great Western and the financial outlook for the years after the war was, therefore, far from satisfactory.

It was clear that the Government could not ignore the matter and in 1919 it decided to retain control of the railways for a further two years after the war ended by means of an Act of Parliament which also established the Ministry of Transport. This breathing space gave time for consideration and after long and difficult negotiations between the Government and the Railway Companies Association – whose chairman during 1920 and 1921 was Lord Churchill, Chairman of the Great Western – the outcome was the Railways Act of 1921. Government control then ceased and the companies resumed the normal management of their businesses.

The principal features of the new Act were the grouping of all significant railway companies into four 'Groups', which afterwards became the four new main line companies – the London, Midland & Scottish Railway, the London & North Eastern Railway, the Southern Railway and the Great Western Railway, the latter being the only one to retain its name, a subject

CONSTITUENT RAILWAYS SOUTH WALES 1921

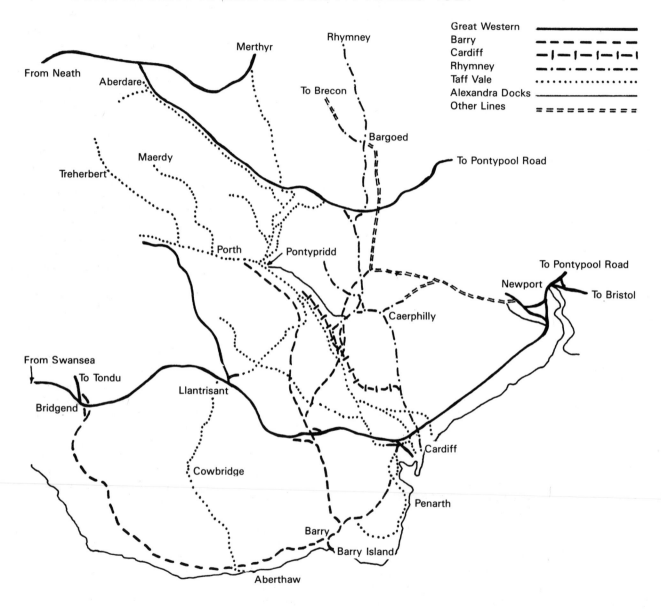

Great Western
Barry
Cardiff
Rhymney
Taff Vale
Alexandra Docks
Other Lines

From Neath
Merthyr
Rhymney
Aberdare
To Brecon
Bargoed
To Pontypool Road
Maerdy
Treherbert
Porth
Pontypridd
To Pontypool Road
Newport
To Bristol
Caerphilly
From Swansea
To Tondu
Llantrisant
Bridgend
Cowbridge
Penarth
Barry
Cardiff
Barry Island
Aberthaw

immortalised by a famous cartoon in the *South Wales News* of 27 November 1922.

The Act specified the 'Constituent Companies' and gave them until 1 January 1923 to prepare voluntary schemes of amalgamation. It also specified 'Subsidiary Companies' which were to be absorbed by the Constituent Companies. In the Western Group all the Constituent Companies, apart from the Great Western itself, were small companies with lines in Wales, so that in practice the GWR was clearly the dominant partner. The Constituent Companies and their mileages were:

Great Western Railway	3,000 miles
Cambrian Railways	295 miles
Taff Vale Railway	124 miles
Barry Railway	68 miles
Rhymney Railway	51 miles
Cardiff Railway	12 miles
Alexandra Docks & Railway	10 miles

Good progress was made and the amalgamation of all these Constituent Companies took effect from 1 January 1922 and at 1 January 1923 agreement had been reached with all but 4 of the 26 Subsidiary Companies. Negotiations with these four were completed later. The fact that the Welsh companies were 'Constituents' enabled them to be represented on the Great Western Board, a move which went a long way to smoothing relationships with the Great Western.

Mr F.J.C. Pole (later Sir Felix), General Manager of the GWR at the time, tells the interesting tale of the behind-the-scenes moves that occurred before and during the passage of the Bill through Parliament. The Minister of Transport, Sir Eric Geddes, issued a White Paper outlining his proposals to reduce the railways from 110 companies to 7, but in later discussion with the Railway Companies Association the number was reduced to 4. Before the Bill was introduced into Parliament the members of the Association were allowed to see it and on the day it was sent to the Great Western Mr Pole was lunching with Sir Philip Nash, one of the Minister's Principal Assistants. The former expressed the view that while it was quite reasonable for such companies as the L&NW, the Midland and the L&Y to be regarded as co-equal Constituent Companies, it was

not reasonable to bracket the Great Western with the five relatively small Welsh companies. He suggested that it would be far better for the Western Group to have the Great Western as the only Constituent Company, leaving it to negotiate terms with the small Welsh companies. Sir Philip thought this was reasonable and suggested that the Great Western should put the idea to the Minister. On Mr Pole's return to Paddington he immediately informed the chairman, Lord Churchill, who wrote at once to Sir Eric Geddes about it. This clearly had the desired effect for when the Bill was introduced into the Commons the Great Western was shown as the only Constituent Company of the Western Group, with the small Welsh companies shown as Subsidiary Companies to be absorbed by it.

During the Committee stage several efforts were made by members to alter the Bill. The LNWR made strenuous efforts to have the Rhymney Railway transferred to the North Western, Midland and Western Scottish Group, doubtless with an eye to access to Cardiff via Rhymney Bridge and the junction there with the Abergavenny to Merthyr line. Other members suggested an entirely separate Group for South Wales, while yet another effort was directed to making the larger of the South Wales companies constituents with the Great Western, rather than Subsidiary Companies.

While the discussions were going on the Minister advised Mr Pole that he felt bound to make some concession to Welsh sentiment and enquired whether the company would object to reverting to the original proposal to make five Welsh companies 'Constituent'. Mr Pole replied that he would not object and, indeed, suggested adding a sixth company to Sir Eric's list provided the other amendments proposed were declined, that the Bill specified that the name of the new Group should be 'Great Western Railway' and that the Great Western Railway Company should not be wound up, as was proposed for all other Constituent Companies.

Sir Eric accepted these suggestions, provided suitable clauses could be drafted to cover the points. The Great Western solicitor set about doing so and the Act duly contained all the protection required to carry on the name of the Great Western Railway for the next 25 years until nationalisation.

A SURVIVAL OF TITLE.

DICK CERMAN

THE GREAT WESTERN: "Hooray! Never even blew me cap off!"

"None of the companies which survive the amalgamation upheaval have come out of it with so much enhanced prestige as the Great Western. It is the only one to retain its old and familiar title."—"South Wales News" leading article.)

Reproduced from the "South Wales News," Monday, November 27, 1922.

The expressive cartoon which appeared in the *South Wales Daily News* on November 27 1922 (*reproduced with permission from the South Wales Echo*)

Chapter Eight

Post War Developments

One important result of the 1923 Grouping was the fact that the Great Western became the owner of the large group of docks in South Wales which had been owned previously by four of the small constituent companies. A new Docks Department was established and this was headed by the former general manager of the Alexandra Docks & Railway Company. During the ensuing years he was responsible for a great deal of investment, mainly directed towards improving the ability to handle the large export coal business efficiently. New sidings and coal loading equipment were provided capable of accommodating 20ton wagons which so improved productivity that the company offered rate rebates to colliery companies which used them.

Co-ordination of traffic, both passenger and freight, was also pursued among the amalgamated companies in East Wales by the setting up of a new Cardiff Valleys Division with a former officer of the Taff Vale company at its head and the locomotive superintendent of the Rhymney Railway in a similar post in the new Division. A new Central Wales Division, based at Oswestry, was also formed to cover the Cambrian, and parts of the Brecon & Merthyr and Neath & Brecon systems.

One of the first major projects to improve train working in South Wales affected the Rhymney Railway whose Cardiff (Parade) station was a short distance from the Taff Vale's Queen Street station. The junctions at the north end of Queen Street were altered to enable Rhymney line trains to run into Queen Street station, whereupon Parade station was closed.

The late 1920s and early 1930s were times of serious economic depression in Great Britain. The General Strike of 1926 made a severe impact upon the finances of the railways although from the first a skeleton service was kept running on the Great Western by loyal staff and volunteers; as each day passed more and more trains were run. Road transport, too, was beginning to make an impact upon rail services and in order to compete more effectively the Great Western extended its own road motor lorry services first introduced in the early 1900s. These country lorry services conveyed goods from railheads to rural areas remote from the railway to a regular timetable. The first Great Western bus service was introduced as early as 1903, between Helston and The Lizard. These services were extended in the ensuing years and in 1928 the Great Western joined with the National Omnibus Company in Devon and Cornwall to form the Western National Omnibus Company. A similar arrangement was made in South Wales with South Wales Commercial Motors and thus the GWR achieved a significant role in the control of bus services in its area. On the railway itself many new halts or unmanned stations were introduced to tap passenger traffic from the smaller rural communities.

But the recession was having its effects by causing serious unemployment by the standards of 1929; in fact, a million people were in this category. However, the Government was seeking ways of reducing the numbers without jobs and passed an Act of Parliament which enabled it to pay the interest on money borrowed by the railways to finance major improvement schemes. The Great Western was quick to take advantage of this legislation and came forward with a number of good schemes, several of them affecting the West of England traffic. Two of the first were the avoiding lines at Westbury and Frome, designed to enable express trains to run through these areas at speed and avoid the time loss caused by speed restrictions – as low as 30mph – through the stations. While a few West of England trains called at Westbury, none did so at Frome and thus the schemes improved journey times and contributed to avoiding congestion, especially on summer Saturdays.

Another important West of England scheme was the reconstruction of Taunton station and quadrupling of the track between Cogload Junction and Norton Fitzwarren on either side of Taunton, a distance of 7½ miles. The principal features were the flyover junction at Cogload where the Bristol and Westbury lines con-

verged and the complicated track layout at North Fitz-warren needed to accommodate the junctions with the lines to Barnstaple and Minehead.

Other major schemes affected principal stations. Improved track layouts and passenger facilities were

Opposite (top) a 2 ton 7 cwt solid tyre bus on the Mathry–St David's service and (bottom) an AEC vehicle of the Country Lorry Service, based at Bedwyn and loaded with empty milk churns (*BR/OPC*). Below a 1950 view shows the junctions at Norton Fitzwarren with the main line straight ahead and the Barnstaple and Minehead branches on the right
Brunel University/R.J. Sellick Collection

provided at Paddington, Bristol and Cardiff General all of which involved, in addition, the installation of colour light signalling with fewer signal boxes in place of the existing semaphore signalling. The freight business was included in other schemes such as the enlargement of marshalling yards at Severn Tunnel Junction and Banbury.

In the field of mechanical engineering other notable developments occurred, spurred on in 1924 by a visit to Swindon Works by King George V and Queen Mary and following which the King drove the Royal Train headed by Castle class locomotive *Windsor Castle* from the Works to Swindon station.

The Castle class, introduced in 1923, was the most powerful locomotive in the country at that time but, more importantly, set new standards for fuel economy which were well ahead of any rivals. In speed too new standards were being set and of this more later. The Castle class represented the top performance that could be achieved within the limitations of a maximum axle load of 20 tons but the time was near when this restriction could be lifted over some of the main routes, principally those to Plymouth, Bristol and Wolverhampton, where both track and bridges had been renewed over a period of years to take higher loadings.

This was the situation which created the opportunity for an even more powerful locomotive, still to the surprise of many of the 4-6-0 type rather than the 4-6-2 wheel arrangement adopted by at least one other company. The result was the majestic King class of which 30

Below, the aircraft used on the GWR's 1931 air service bearing the company's crest on the tailplane. Opposite (top) *King George V*, complete with Red Indian and Westinghouse brake, is pictured on its United States tour and (below) a GWR railcar is at work on the Cardiff–Birmingham service   *BR/OPC*

were built at Swindon from 1927 onwards. It was intended originally to name the class after cathedrals but a significant event caused a change of mind. The Baltimore & Ohio Railroad in the United States was celebrating its centenary in 1927 and invited the Great Western to send over a modern locomotive. Doubtless the Americans would regard it as a national rather than a purely Great Western exhibit and it was felt, therefore, that a more appropriate name was required. With the gracious consent of His Majesty the first of the new locomotives was named *King George V* and thereafter the whole class became the 'Kings'. It was a master stroke of Great Western publicity, of which there were many examples during Sir Felix Pole's time as general manager.

The Great Western had been looking carefully at the merits of diesel traction for railcars and in 1933 introduced one experimentally for local services between Paddington and Oxford. It was so successful that the following year more powerful railcars were introduced on a new express service between Cardiff and Birmingham, stopping only at Newport and Gloucester. These provided two services a day in each direction, at times convenient to businessmen, and included a small buffet counter at one end in addition to seating for 40 third class passengers. The author can well recall, as a schoolboy, the thrill of travelling at 75mph in one of these cars, and especially the novelty of being able to view the track through end windows.

The British main line railways had obtained Parliamentary powers to run air services in 1929 and the Great Western became the first to exercise these powers when, in 1931, it introduced an air service between Cardiff and Plymouth, with an intermediate call at Haldon Aerodrome to serve Teignmouth and Torquay. Special buses connected the aerodromes and the railway stations and the air service was run in conjunction with Imperial Airways who provided a 6-seater Westland Wessex plane painted in GWR chocolate and cream and furnished internally to the standard of a first class carriage. The following year the service was extended to Birmingham.

As the 1930s progressed the railways were becoming increasingly concerned at the rising price of coal of which they were, of course, large users as well as large carriers. They were also worried by the rapid development of road freight transport which was seen as unfair competition in that the railways were common carriers whose methods of fixing rates were regulated by statute, whereas the road hauliers could pick and choose the traffic they carried and fix their own rates for doing so. This situation resulted in the 'Square Deal' campaign of 1938 which was aimed at persuading the Government to release the railways from these restrictive obligations. It had some effect because the Minister of Transport set up a Transport Advisory Council which reported in May 1939 and favoured some relaxation of the regulations governing the railway companies. Unfortunately, war clouds were looming and more important matters caused further consideration of the report to be postponed.

To revert to the price of coal, the problems for the Great Western were compounded by the long haul over steep gradients to depots in the West of England and the Board considered that there might, therefore, be economies to be realised by electrifying the main line west of Taunton. In 1938 they commissioned a well known firm of consulting engineers to investigate the matter and report on its feasibility and financial benefits. The report, issued in 1939, was based on overhead electrification at 3,000 volts D.C. and while it demonstrated savings of about 18% per annum in working costs, the return on capital was as low as 1% and the Board therefore decided not to proceed. One of the main reasons for the low return was the additional cost caused by the predominance of sharp curves, especially west of Exeter, which required overhead masts to be at closer than normal spacing to ensure that locomotive pantographs always registered correctly on the overhead wire.

No doubt, in the circumstances, the decision was a correct one and, for the civil engineer, avoided the additional restraint on permanent way maintenance that overhead wires represent, for he cannot adjust the alignment or level of the track beyond very fine limits without the co-operation of the electrical engineer. That is not to say that electrification should be resisted, but rather that it needs to be recognised that permanent way maintenance 'under the wires' becomes more complicated and more costly.

Chapter Nine

Centenary Year

The Great Western Railway Act received the Royal Assent on 31 August 1835 and so the year 1935 was unique in that it enabled the Great Western to celebrate its centenary while still in existence and with the knowledge that no other British main line railway was ever likely to do the same. It was not the first railway centenary to be celebrated, however, since 1925 had seen special events to commemorate the opening of the Stockton & Darlington Railway in 1825 and in 1930 there had been more celebrations to recall the opening of the Liverpool & Manchester Railway. The Great Western had taken part in both of these events but in 1935 the occasion was its own and it celebrated in style.

The 31st of August 1935 was a Saturday and the day was marked by a Celebration Lunch in the Great Hall of Bristol University. A special train for the party of London guests left Paddington at 10 o'clock and reached Bristol two hours later. On arrival the chairman, Sir Robert Horne, accompanied by the Rt Hon J.H. Thomas, Dominions Secretary and a former Great Western man, were greeted by the Sheriff of Bristol and proceeded to call on the Lord Mayor at the Council House. From there they all travelled in the Lord Mayor's coach to the University.

After the Lord Mayor of Bristol had proposed the toast of 'The Great Western Railway Company' the chairman replied and described the occasion as one 'to stir the memory and inspire the imagination'. In his speech he also announced that a new express, *The Bristolian*, would be introduced on the 9th of September and would run non-stop between Paddington and Bristol in 1¾ hours – 15 minutes faster than any existing service and at an average speed of 67mph. Furthermore, as a foretaste of that development, the train taking the guests back to London would run in the exact times of the new service, leaving Bristol at 4.30pm. It was hauled by a King class locomotive, *King George V*, with six special saloons and a kitchen car and the smoothness of the run was commented upon, especially as those taking tea did not find it spilled in their saucers – a rough test, even today, as to the quality of ride experienced at speeds much higher than those of *The Bristolian*.

Before returning to Paddington the guests were

6013 King Henry VIII on
The Bristolian
BR/OPC

The replica *North Star* as it appeared in the GWR Centenary
Film   *BR/OPC*

shown the special centenary film for which a full size
replica of the locomotive *North Star* and carriages of the
broad gauge era had been built.The film was also shown
to groups of staff and their friends and as a boy the
author was fortunate enough to see it at a showing in the
Staff Association building near Queen Street station at
Cardiff.

Another audience which saw the centenary film was
the guests at the great Centenary Banquet held at Gros-
venor House in London on 30 October. The principal
guest was the Prince of Wales (later King Edward VIII)
and 1,100 other guests were present, including MPs and
the Lord Mayors and Mayors of cities and towns served
by the Great Western, representatives of trade and
industry, the trade unions and also officers of the company and elected representatives of the staff.

In proposing the toast of 'The Great Western Railway
Company', His Royal Highness said, "Your great
Company deserves its name of 'The Royal Road' if only
for the fact that it was on your wheels that Queen
Victoria first experienced railroad travel and because it
was on your lines that she was borne on her last journey

home". He was, of course, referring to the Queen's first railway journey between Slough and Paddington in 1842 and to the Royal funeral train between Paddington and Windsor in 1901. Sir Robert Horne in reply said, "I feel the greatest possible diffidence in replying to the charming speech that has just been delivered. The Prince of Wales has blown us a blast from a great trumpet and I am sorry that I can only reply with a feeble horn!"

The Press, both technical and national, paid great attention to the centenary events. The *Railway Gazette* issued a special centenary number and *The Times* issued a special 28-page supplement on 31 August, dealing with all aspects of the GWR's activities. The BBC, too, broadcast a special programme on 30 August. It followed an imaginary journey from Paddington to Penzance via Bristol, outlining the beginnings of the Great Western, the construction of its lines, the extensive changes that had occurred since and, by interviewing a number of railwaymen, demonstrated the daily tasks involved in running and maintaining such a complex undertaking. In the leading article of its supplement, *The Times* described the GWR as 'a lively organism of infinite complexity, made simple by the aim to which the energies and resources of all Departments are bent in the service of the travelling public.' Such tributes were not easily earned, but were well deserved.

The final gesture to mark the centenary was the provision of two completely new sets of coaches for the company's most important train the *Cornish Riviera Express*, affectionately known as 'The Limited' in view of its load being strictly limited to seven coaches when first introduced in 1904. The new vehicles were luxurious in their interior fittings and as wide as the Great Western loading gauge would allow – 9ft 7ins overall – which precluded their use on other railways. But luxury too has progressed in the past fifty years and the *Cornish Riviera* express today is worked by an Inter-City 125 High Speed Train with modern air conditioned coaches and whereas in 1935 the journey time for the 226 miles from Paddington to Plymouth was 4 hours, it has now been reduced to 3 hours exactly.

The centenary coaches built for the *Cornish Riviera Express*, the appearance of which is not really enhanced by the GWR's concessions to locomotive streamlining *BR/OPC*

Chapter Ten

World War II and Nationalisation

As in World War I, so in World War II very heavy demands were made on the railways for carrying both passengers and freight. But this time there was a difference for in the intervening twenty years the development of air power had been such that the railway system was in serious danger of disruption at the hands of enemy bombers. Right at the start of the war the Government again took control of the railways with a Railway Executive chaired this time, not by a Minister, but by the recently-retired Chief General Manager of the LNER and with the general managers of the main line companies as members.

There were long arguments with the Government about the compensation to be paid to the companies, bearing in mind that they had maintained their assets in first rate condition up to the outbreak of war and were then expected to carry considerably more traffic. In fact it was not until 7 February 1940 that the Minister issued a White Paper on the subject which was reluctantly accepted by the companies. The agreed arrangements involved pooling all revenues and expenses of the four main line railways and London Transport, and distributing a guaranteed minimum sum which was the average of the net revenue for the years 1935–6–7. For the Great Western this represented approximately 16% of the pool. Any surplus over the guaranteed minimum, up to a total of £3.5m, was to be distributed in the same proportions as the guaranteed minimum itself. After this any further net revenues accrued to the Government.

This time the passenger train service was drastically thinned out right at the beginning and a maximum speed limit of 60mph was imposed, although later in the war this was relaxed to 75mph. The initial lower figure had been influenced by the possible effect of air raid damage.

An immediate task for the Great Western was the evacuation of schoolchildren and their teachers to various country destinations – mainly from London but also from other big cities. All this had been planned well in advance and the London operation was based on Ealing Broadway, to which the children were conveyed by London Transport. Fifty trains of a standard 12-coach formation were ear-marked, concentrated at Old Oak Common and Acton yards, and called forward to Ealing for departures between 8.30am and 5.30pm at nine minute intervals. The destinations of most were in the West Country and to accommodate all this extra traffic the normal passenger service from Paddington was drastically reduced and confined entirely to the main lines between Paddington and Reading during the four days that the special operation was in progress. Smooth working of the plan depended not only on the punctual supply of trains to Ealing Broadway but also upon London Transport delivering the parties of children to Ealing at the right time. It was a triumph of good organisation and worked splendidly.

The GWR office staff at Paddington were moved to sites in Berkshire west of Reading, some departments taking over country houses and a large number of others moving into newly-erected sheds at Aldermaston. When railway staff returned to Paddington after the war the sheds were taken over by Sterling Cables who still occupy them.

Railway traffic quickly built up and was worked with great difficulty under blackout conditions and, not infrequently, under air attack. There were a considerable number of bombing incidents, including two at Paddington station itself. In one of these part of the Down Side offices was demolished and in the other there was damage to the station roof and platforms.

Many were the heroic deeds of the staff, of whom 68 were killed on duty, but perhaps the most notable of all occurred in the Great Western freight yard at Birkenhead. The Germans were dropping incendiary bombs on Merseyside and several dropped on a train loaded with high explosive bombs which was ready to depart. One incendiary fell on an open wagon covered with a

World War II bomb damage at Paddington *British Rail*

tarpaulin and then burned through it, becoming wedged between two 250lb bombs. A shunter, Norman Tunna, ran to the engine to get a bucket of water but when that failed to extinguish the fire he tried a stirrup pump. The driver of the train, W.T. Davies and his fireman F.R. Newns helped in dealing with the situation but by then the blaze had become too fierce and, if an explosion was to be averted, radical action was needed. At this point Mr Tunna climbed into the wagon, prised the bombs apart with his shunting pole and then lifted out the incendiary with his bare hands and threw it clear.

For his act of selfless devotion and bravery Norman Tunna was awarded the George Cross. Both Davies and Newns were awarded the George Medal for their part in averting what could have been a serious explosion with much loss of life. It is fitting that Tunna's bravery is still recalled by a Class 47 diesel locomotive which bears his name.

In preparation for the repair of damage from air attack the Great Western engineering department had stock piled materials such as military trestling, heavy timber piling and trackwork, including crossovers. However the main damage which occurred was not widely known to the public for security reasons and some of the incidents were not disclosed until the war was over.

The engineering department was also involved in the provision of a number of short connecting lines to open up new routes for diversionary purposes in the event of air raid damage. A good example is the Hawkeridge curve at Westbury which enabled trains for Bristol and South Wales to run in emergency via Newbury and, avoiding reversal at Westbury station, to regain the Bristol main line at Bathampton. This line has been retained since the war and is still used for diversionary purposes.

No story of the Great Western's war effort would be complete without reference to the important part played by their ships from both the Irish and Channel Islands routes. Of the five passenger ferries, four were requisitioned by the Government – the *St Andrew*, *St David* and *St Julien* as hospital ships and the *St Helier* as a troop transport. All played a most distinguished part in the evacuation of the British Expeditionary Force from Dunkirk. Their GWR masters and crews showed almost superhuman gallantry in the face of heavy enemy attacks with both bombs and artillery and yet, in that operation, suffered no serious damage or casualties.

The evacuation of troops from Dunkirk gave the railways one of their sternest tests in moving, at very short notice, over 330,000 men from the South Coast ports to various destinations in the country. Many of these were either on the Great Western or involved passing through Great Western territory to other railways. A total of 160 sets of coaches, 40 of them from the GWR, were provided and during the seven days of the operation 293 special trains were run over the Great Western, conveying a total of over 180,000 men.

During World War II railway service was a reserved occupation. Nevertheless numbers of Great Western men had army commitments in the Territorials and the Supplementary Reserve and other young men were called up as hostilities progressed. The total number of Great Western staff serving in the Forces was about 15,000, of whom 600 lost their lives. By the end of the war no fewer than 89 had been awarded medals for meritorious war service.

At the end of the war the railways were retained under Government control and at the General Election of 1945 the electorate returned a Labour Government committed to widespread nationalisation. This created two years of uncertainty until the Bill nationalising all forms of public inland transport, except air transport, received the Royal Assent on 6 August 1947. It created the British Transport Commission whose first chairman was Sir Cyril Hurcombe, a distinguished civil servant, and the new organisation came into operation on 1 January 1948. The four railway companies were reorganised into six Regions – Eastern, London Midland, North Eastern, Southern, Western and Scottish, the latter comprising those parts of the LMS and LNE Railways north of the border, while the Eastern and North Eastern Regions were formed from the Southern and North Eastern areas respectively of the LNER.

The other Regions started with the same territory as the companies they replaced in England and Wales. The new organisation was functional, with each departmental head reporting to his departmental chief in a Railway Executive which was one of a number of Executives for the different forms of transport reporting to the Commission. Each Region was headed by a Chief Regional Officer to co-ordinate the various Regional departments.

And so, from the end of 1947, the Great Western Railway Company ceased to control its assets after a life of 112 years. The final General Meeting was held at Paddington on 5 March 1948; it lasted only twenty minutes, approved a final dividend of 7.28% and, with the Meeting over, the company's formal business came to an end.

The Great Western's successor, the Western Region, retained that independence of mind which characterised the GWR over so many years. It is a feature which exists to the present day and long may it remain so!

Chapter Eleven

More Great Western Personalities

To the present day the Great Western Railway and the Western Region has always had able men to run its affairs and to single out for special comment some of the outstanding personalities has not been easy. However, four have been selected, unhappily none of them still alive. The four are Viscount Churchill, Chairman from 1908 to 1934, Sir Felix Pole, General Manager from 1921 to 1929, Mr G.J. Churchward, Locomotive & Carriage Superintendent and later Chief Mechanical Engineer from 1902 to 1921 and finally Sir Allan Quartermaine, Chief Engineer from 1940 to 1951. In making the selection it must not be assumed that others are unworthy of comment, but rather that space is limited and no doubt history will record, in due course, the oustanding service of those still in office and more recently retired.

Viscount Churchill joined the Great Western Board in 1905 and became chairman early in 1908. He has the distinction of being the longest serving chairman of the company, serving for almost 26 years until he died in 1934. The only other chairman to approach his record was Sir Daniel Gooch who served for 24 years. Churchill had earlier been a soldier and politician and brought to the Great Western a rare, all-round ability to inspire loyalty and give able guidance. He was renowned for his unfailing courtesy and charming manners which, coupled with a sympathetic ear, endeared him to officers and staff alike. But he was also a good businessman, guiding the company through many difficult periods and able to deal with criticism impartially, which found him defending the company's policy relentlessly when appropriate but, at the same time, insisting upon change when such was clearly necessary. Under his brilliant leadership the Great Western became one of the principal transport undertakings in the country.

Felix Pole joined the Great Western in the Telegraph Department at Swindon in 1891 at the age of 14 and after three years was transferred to Paddington where he spent the rest of his service. After six years in the chief engineer's office he was promoted to the general manager's office where he spent some years on personnel and trade union matters as secretary to the company's side of the GWR Conciliation Boards, and also as editor of the Great Western Railway Magazine. After this he progressed quickly and became General Manager in 1921. He was one of the most 'go ahead' general managers the company had had. His energy and industry were limitless and his tenacity of purpose overcame all

THE RT. HON. VISCOUNT CHURCHILL, G.C.V.O.

Devon and Great Western amalgamated in 1876. After six years in the drawing office Churchward was appointed assistant manager of the Carriage Works and later, manager of the Locomotive Works. In 1902 he was appointed to the top post in his department, which he occupied for over nineteen years and which, from 1916, was designated Chief Mechanical Engineer. He was a leading authority on locomotive practice and his adoption of the standardisation of parts, including boilers, revolutionised the procedures previously used and reduced significantly the cost of repairs. He was also renowned for his use of superheaters for the boilers in all but small shunting locomotives, which made his 4-cylinder express passenger locomotives outstanding in performance compared with those of other companies.

Sir Felix Pole, General Manager, Great Western Railway 1921–9   *BR/OPC*

G.J. Churchward, Chief Mechanical Enginer, Great Western Railway 1902–21   *BR/OPC*

obstacles. It has been said that he possessed a practical mind, sound judgement and a quick grasp of problems, a wonderful memory, remarkable foresight and great tact. Surely enough to mark him out as a truly great General Manager; and his knighthood in 1924 came as no surprise. Pole had no thought of leaving the Great Western, but in 1929 he was tempted by an offer from industry to become chairman of Associated Electrical Industries and the GWR lost a most distinguished servant. He was succeeded, fortunately, by his able deputy James Milne, who presided until nationalisation in 1948 and was himself knighted in 1931.

George Jackson Churchward was a Devonian who started his railway career as a pupil on the South Devon Railway and was moved to Swindon when the South

Churchward was also prominent in local government in Swindon and was chairman of New Swindon Urban District Council in 1897 and the first Mayor of the new Borough of Swindon in 1900. He retired in 1921 and his death came tragically in 1933 when he was run down by the Fishguard Express outside the grounds of his home which adjoined the line at Swindon.

Finally, mention must be made of a great civil engineer, under whom the author was privileged to serve – Allan Quartermaine, later Sir Allan. After graduating at London University with First Class Honours, he received practical training with Hertfordshire County Council and the Teeside Bridge & Engineering Company and then joined the Great Western Railway in the divisional engineer's office at Wolverhampton in 1910. Surprisingly, he resigned in 1911 but soon saw the error of his ways and rejoined the service again at Wolverhampton the following year. Three years later he moved to Paddington as an Assistant in the chief engineer's office and saw war service in Egypt with the Royal Engineers where he attained the rank of Major and was awarded the Military Cross. On his return to England he was soon appointed Assistant Divisional Engineer at Gloucester, to be followed by three years as Divisonal Engineer at Bristol. Then, after ten years as Assistant Chief Engineer and Deputy Chief Engineer of the GWR, he became head of his department in January 1940.

Quartermaine had not been in office for many months before he was seconded to the Government as Director General of Aircraft Production Factories and his predecessor took over as Acting Chief Engineer during his absence, which lasted until January 1941. On his return Quartermaine was not only involved with the difficult task of maintaining the railway with much-reduced wartime resources, but also with the repair of bomb damage and, perhaps almost as difficult, the rehabilitation of track and structures to their pre-war standards after the war was over.

Sir Allan Quartermaine was a most able engineer and administrator and the author was privileged to be his personal assistant during his last year of office, in which he was elected President of the Institution of Civil Engineers. A still vivid memory is his orderly way of working and insistence that the 4-weekly statements showing the various facets of departmental progress should be on his desk by the dates he specified. He was awarded the CBE in 1943 and was knighted in 1956.

Sir Allan Quartermaine, Chief Civil Enginer, Great Western Railway 1940–7 *British Rail*

Chapter Twelve

Modernisation and Organisation

Since nationalisation the railways have seldom been outside the political arena and their fortunes have been dictated to a considerable extent by the government of the day. Governments of both main parties have tended to be tough in their financial oversight of railways and rather less tough with roads, vast millions being invested in the latter to an extent which makes railwaymen envious. In fairness, however, it must be said that there have recently been welcome signs of a more favourable attitude by Government towards railways.

After World War II the railways had become run down and the great Modernisation Plan of 1955 was seen as the means of revitalising them. One of the plan's principal ingredients was the electrification of several suburban services and also one or two busy main lines, principally the West Coast Main Line of the London Midland Region, but none on the Western Region. For the Western it was the demise of the steam locomotive and its replacement by a much smaller number of diesel locomotives and diesel multiple unit railcars that formed the major part of the plan. This involved a gradual changeover covering almost ten years with the steady elimination of steam engine sheds and their substitution with significantly fewer diesel maintenance depots and inspection and fuelling points.

The Western Region alone decided on hydraulic rather than electrical transmission for its new diesel locomotives. This was based on a successful German design but, unfortunately, with experience under the higher speed and intensity of British operating conditions the diesel hydraulic locomotives proved to be more expensive to maintain than the diesel electric types in use on other Regions and in the 1970s they were gradually phased out as changing traffic patterns and higher productivity permitted a reduction in the total numbers of locomotives required.

On the freight side there was to be major expenditure in providing large hump marshalling yards and a significant reduction in the number of flat yards, together with

A Type 4 Warship diesel hydraulic locomotive at Twyford
British Rail

the fitting of continuous brakes to all freight wagons to enable freight trains to run safely at much higher speeds. The mechanical engineers proposed to use the air brake in view of its superior performance, but it was not adopted by the Board because of strong objections by the operating departments of the Regions who feared the problems of having both vacuum and air brakes in use at the same time. With hindsight the decision appears to have been rather short-sighted and it was reversed some years later so that today new builds of both passenger and freight rolling stock are air braked. There are, of course, still some passenger vehicles which are vacuum-fitted, as also are a number of freight vehicles, although these are gradually being phased out. However, it is likely to be a few years yet before the last vacuum-fitted vehicles finally disappear.

A major marshalling yard at Margam near Port Talbot was already being built and, as part of the Modernisation Plan, others were planned at Brookthorpe near Gloucester and Walcot near Shrewsbury. Fortunately they were never built, as the gradual reduction of traditional wagon load traffic coupled with the new high capacity, fast through service concept made these unnecessary. Even Margam has now been drastically reduced in size and has reverted to a flat yard.

Both before and during the implementation of the Modernisation Plan organisational changes had been taking place. Indeed, to one much of whose career spanned the years since nationalisation, it has seemed that there has rarely been a year when reorganisation has not either been planned or in progress, with an increasing amount of management time being devoted to it. A well known general manager of the Region, Gerard Fiennes, once said, "When you reorganise, you bleed." How true; the balance between adjusting to changing circumstances and maintaining effective management continuity is not easy to strike.

An important reorganisation took place in the late 1950s with the creation of four traffic divisions with headquarters at Paddington, Birmingham, Bristol and Cardiff, the last three having subordinate district organisations. This alteration, however, left unsolved the problem of Western and London Midland routes in the Midlands. These were very intertwined and required a drastic solution to unscramble. It also left unsolved the situation in Devon and Cornwall where both Western and Southern routes existed and required rationalisation.

The solution to the Midlands problem came in 1963 and involved the transfer to the London Midland Region not only of the Western lines in the Birmingham area but also the line from Ardley, about 10 miles south of Banbury, right through to Saltney on the outskirts of Chester and including all the Western Region branches in Wales from Aberystwyth northwards. At the time the author was District Engineer at Shrewsbury and did not immediately appreciate the change, but the LMR welcomed the newcomers and set about integrating them into their ways of working.

The London Midland Region reorganised into Divisions later than the Western and in 1966 the ex-Western territory was brought within the new LM Divisional reorganisation, which involved the closure of the former WR Birmingham Division and Shrewsbury District of the Wales Division. At the same time the civil engineering districts were reorganised into divisions which had territories coterminous with the traffic divisions.

These changes opened the way for solving the Devon and Cornwall problem. Here a new Plymouth Division was formed in 1963 from the former Exeter and Plymouth Districts of the Bristol Division and the former Southern Region Exeter District. The latter had been retained by the Western when the SR line between Wilton, 2½ miles west of Salisbury, and Exeter together with the lines west of Exeter were transferred to the Western in that year. An important result of this reorganisation was the decision to make the Westbury route the principal one from London to the West of England with only a semi-fast service on the ex-Southern route which was singled except for the section between Templecombe and Yeovil Junction.

One of the early roles of the WR divisions was to play a major part in the line closure programme of the era when Dr Beeching was Board Chairman. The Western was affected significantly and apart from the London area, Cornwall and South Wales very few branch lines remained. Indeed, most of the former Southern lines in Devon and Cornwall were closed and, finally, the recently-formed divisional office at Plymouth suffered the same fate.

Regional boundary changes, it seems, are never complete and as recently as 1981 the part of the Salisbury–Exeter line between Wilton and Sherborne was transferred back to the Southern Region for reasons of signalling and operation in connection with the new panel signalling control centre at Salisbury. At the same time and for the same reasons the part of the Westbury–Salisbury line between Dilton Marsh and Heytesbury was transferred back to the Western Region and came under the control of the new Westbury panel box.

The largest reorganisation of all, however, was proposed by the British Railways Board in 1971 following investigations by consultants McKinsey & Co. This was known as the 'Field Reorganisation' and involved splitting the system into eight 'territories' of which the Western was to be one, fortunately with virtually unchanged boundaries. However, on the basis that the bulk of the Region's commercial activity was centred around the Bristol Channel and taking into account the Board's wish to decentralise management away from Central London, the new headquarters was to be at Cardiff in Brunel House, a newly-built office block adjoining Queen Street station. The proposals involved elimination of the traffic divisions with movement of salaried staff on a vast scale and, not unnaturally, the trade unions were unhappy at such a prospect.

After a considerable expenditure of management time in shaping the new organisation it was decided in 1975 to abandon it and to reorganise less drastically and at a slower pace. So, with many sighs of relief from managers and staff alike, the traffic divisions survived, but only for a few years and then only with their responsibilities being gradually diminished with the centralisation at regional headquarters of the mechanical & electrical engineering and the freight commercial functions. Finally, in early 1984, they were abolished altogether and replaced by a direct management line from regional headquarters, now centred at Swindon, to the area managers. Thus, after more then a century, the permanent location of general management moved away from Paddington.

Throughout all this upheaval the civil engineering function, which under the Field Organisation was to be split into seven areas, had been reorganised into five Divisions, now designated 'Areas', based at Reading, Bristol, Exeter, Newport and Swansea. While the geographical spread of track and structures to be maintained remains substantially the same, it will continue to meet the Region's needs. Up until 1984 the headquarters office for the function remained at Paddington but a decision was then taken that it should move to Swindon during the following year.

Type 4 Western No. 1002 *Western Explorer* with a parcels train at Taplow in 1962   *British Rail*

Chapter Thirteen

High Speed

High speed is a relative term and in the early days of railways even 40mph was considered to be fast. The Great Western, however, was determined to make good use of its broad gauge and before long speeds of 60mph were being achieved. Indeed, it is recorded that in 1852 Queen Victoria became alarmed when told that on one of her journeys she had been travelling at 60mph and commanded her equerry to write to the Great Western asking that they should not allow royal trains to make up any lost time by travelling faster than the speeds implied in the timetable supplied to the Queen.

In those early years an express train was defined as one which ran throughout its journey at a minimum average speed of 40mph including intermediate stops. As early as 1845 a train was running from Paddington to Exeter, via Bristol of course, with seven intermediate stops in 4½ hours and at an average speed of 43mph, but it was 1871 before this time was reduced to 4¼ hours. In 1896 it became 3¾ hours and in 1903, 3½ hours – an average speed of 55mph. At the time the shorter route via Westbury was introduced the time had come down to 3 hours, but over the reduced distance the average speed had increased only to 58mph. By 1939 the best train did the run in 2 hours 50 minutes bringing the average speed to 61mph, but this run was non-stop. In contrast the best non-stop time today is 2 hours 3 minutes by HST at an average speed of almost 85mph. Such is progress.

The story of high speed on the Western as a whole is generally similar with the number of trains averaging 50mph or over increasing from nine in 1888 to fifty four in 1901, and by the 1920s trains averaging over 60mph were running. From the early years of the century, however, there have been a number of special runs of exceptional quality. Several were by non-stop trains from Plymouth Millbay Docks to Paddington in connection with the Atlantic liners which anchored off Plymouth and transferred their passengers and mail to GWR tenders which landed them at Millbay Docks.

The best known of these runs was in May 1904 when the famous locomotive *City of Truro* hauled a train between Plymouth and Bristol at an average speed of 62mph; but the highlight of this journey was the sprint down Wellington Bank, between Exeter and Taunton, where a speed of 102mph was reached! This was not the only Western steam locomotive known to have reached 100mph and there are at least two more.

The first instance was on the Oxford–Worcester line down Campden Bank, between Moreton-in-Marsh and Evesham, in July 1939 when Driver Tidball of Worcester on locomotive 4086 *Builth Castle* reached exactly 100mph with the 12.45pm Paddington to Worcester train. For the record, the load was seven coaches totalling 243 tons.

The second was in the mid-1950s by the *Bristolian* but details were, unfortunately, not recorded beyond the fact of reaching exactly 100mph down Dauntsey Bank, between Swindon and Chippenham. The author was at the rear of the train aboard the Region's Track Testing Car which is equipped with a speedometer, and can vouch for the speed and recall that the locomotive was a 'Castle'.

Such runs were exceptional but showed what could be achieved under ideal conditions. Although not in the 100mph class, mention must be made of a world beating run by the 3.48pm train from Swindon to Paddington one day in June 1932. Driver Ruddock and Fireman Thorpe of Old Oak Common on locomotive 5006 *Tregenna Castle* ran the 77¼ miles between Swindon and Paddington in a fraction under 57 minutes, an average speed of nearly 82mph. Two well-known experts on train timing were aboard and such was the confidence of the Great Western that on the same day it also staged a specially fast run by the 5pm Paddington to Cheltenham, this time with the gradient slightly against the train. The same experts returned to Swindon by this train which reached there in 60 minutes 1 second and in good time to allow them to return to Paddington again

by the 5.15pm express from Bristol which normally slipped a coach at Swindon but on this occasion was specially stopped. In spite of the extra stop and a slight signal check near Didcot, the train still reached Paddington 2½ minutes early.

Before considering present day high speeds, a record of another kind must be noted. In 1904 the Great Western introduced a new express between Paddington and Penzance, the *Cornish Riviera Express* which again ran via Bristol and covered the 246 miles between Paddington and Plymouth non-stop. This was the longest non-stop train journey in the world, an achievement which remained unsurpassed for nearly a quarter of a century. The journey time was 4 hours 27 minutes, which gave an average speed of 55mph. The former was reduced to 4 hours 7 minutes after the Westbury route was opened and to an even 4 hours in 1927 when the greater power of the King class locomotives became available. At the time of writing this chapter the *Cornish Riviera* express, now an HST, reaches Plymouth in 3 hours including a stop at Exeter.

The major step forward to still higher speeds was the introduction of the 'High Speed' diesel trains on the routes to Bristol and Swansea in October 1976. In order to avoid the effect of heavy axle loads on the track at 125mph it was decided to provide two locomotives – or power cars, as they are known since they also include a small van for parcels and mail. On the Western Region the trains comprise seven coaches with a power car at each end and were the first scheduled trains in this country to run at speeds over 100mph.

This was where Brunel's superb alignment and flat gradients of the original Bristol route came into their own and today 125mph is permitted from the 4½ mile-post at Acton right through to the eastern mouth of Box

Tunnel, 99 miles from Paddington, with only two restrictions of speed en route – 80mph through Reading and 100mph through Swindon. On the South Wales route 125mph is permitted as far as Bristol Parkway but with some further restrictions, the lowest (apart from 70mph through Wootton Bassett Junction) being 100mph, mainly due to track curvature. In the 2½-mile long Sodbury Tunnel a slight reduction of speed to 120mph is for aerodynamic reasons to avoid the severe pressure on coach windows which could occur when two trains pass each other inside the tunnel. Originally the permitted speed inside the tunnel was only 110mph and the increase of 10mph was arranged following practical tests and research carried out by the Board's Research & Development Department at Derby.

Before the HSTs could run at these very high speeds, which involved taking a step into the unknown, a considerable amount of work had to be done to upgrade the track. In addition to reballasting about 96 miles of the track, renewing the formation and ballast over a further 12 miles and renewing or overhauling 37 miles of drains, there were eight sites where surveys indicated that major work was required to adjust the curvature to allow 125mph. Perhaps the most interesting of these were at Twyford and Thingley Junction, near Chippenham.

At Twyford the relief lines are straight while the main lines on the south side curve around the island platform between them, and the permitted speed here was only 90mph due in part to an arched road overbridge immediately east of the platforms. The opening of this bridge was widened and both main line platform walls rebuilt to allow the curvature to be flattened to permit 125mph.

At Thingley Junction the problem was a little different. Here the curve was already flat enough for 125mph but there was a facing junction in the Down line diverging from the back of the curve and the increase in cant necessary to raise the speed from 90mph to 125mph would have caused an adverse cant in the diverging junction beyond the permitted limit. The solution to this problem was to create a short straight section containing the junction by sharpening the curves on either side. With a heavy cant on the latter 125mph could be permitted while, at the same time, easing the

Twyford looking west and with the main lines, now suitable for 125 mph, on the left *Author*

maintenance of the junction by placing it on the straight. This same straight was used in the Up line to contain the trailing connection leading to some sidings.

The HSTs started in timetabled service in October 1976 and average start-to-stop speeds of over 90mph became commonplace. Indeed, by the May 1984 timetable there were many such runs but the fastest of all were the 16.00 and 17.20 Paddington to Swansea, these running non-stop to Bristol Parkway a distance of 111¾ miles in 66 minutes, an average speed of 101mph. As with steam, so with HSTs there have been a few special runs at exceptionally fast average speeds. The record belongs to a special HST formed of only five coaches and two power cars which on 30 August 1984 ran the 117½ miles from Paddington to Bristol (Temple Meads) via Badminton in 62 minutes 33 seconds at an average speed of 112.9mph. The special train conveyed Jimmy Savile to Bristol for the naming of one of the power cars (43002) *Top of the Pops*.

A world-beating run with a booked HST passenger train was made on 10 April 1979 when the 09.20 Paddington to Bristol ran the 94 miles to Chippenham non-

GWR Automatic Train Control equipment   *BR/OPC*

ceedings the telephone rang and the Bristol divisional manager, then Mr W. Kent who was obviously expecting the call, answered it to receive the news that the record had been achieved. On returning to his seat it was a dramatic moment when he announced the news to a rather surprised general manager.

Even these high speeds were not the highest ever achieved on the Western for in the summer of 1976 the Board allocated the experimental Advanced Passenger Train to the Region for trials at speeds up to 150mph. It was a tribute to the excellence of the WR track and the stretch chosen for the tests was between Swindon and Reading or, to be more precise, between Uffington and Pangbourne. Here, on Sundays and under special arrangements by which no other train was to pass or be passed by the APT (even on the 4-track section east of Didcot) when running at speed, it was put through its paces and achieved a maximum speed of 152mph. The author travelled on one of the runs when a maximum of 149.8mph was attained and can testify to the satisfactory riding of the coaches at this very high speed.

But with high speed must go safety and the Great Western and Western Region was and is a very safe railway. In the days of steam traction and mechanical signalling especially, staff discipline played an important part in safety even more than it does today but there was one device – invented by and used until after nationalisation only to any extent on the Western – which had a considerable bearing on this good record. It was known as Automatic Train Control and was first tried, in its initial form, on the Henley branch as early as 1906. The system involved a long ramp fixed in the track and which, in conjunction with a plunger on the locomotive, repeated the aspect of the distant signal in the cab. A bell rang if the distant signal was 'off' or showing green – and thus, by interlocking, so were the subsequent stop signals controlled by the same signal box. If the distant signal was 'on' or showing a yellow aspect a siren sounded in the locomotive cab and the brakes were automatically applied.

The ATC device was gradually extended over the principal passenger lines and gave drivers a lot of confidence, especially in bad weather when the oil-lit signals were difficult to see. Since nationalisation a modified system (now known as the Automatic Warning

stop in 50 minutes 31 seconds, a world record average speed of 111.7mph.

While this spectacular 1979 event was a specially planned run with a regularly booked train, it was kept secret even from the general manager. On that particular day his management conference was in session and the author was present, along with the other chief officers and the divisional managers. During the pro-

System) using magnets in place of the ramp has been designed by the British Railways Board and is now extensively used on other Regions in addition to the Western.

With modern technology, especially applied to signalling, the human element in accidents has been reduced and perhaps the driver now has the greatest responsibility in the safe working of trains. However, it must not be forgotten that the permanent way men carry a heavy burden of responsibility since any failure to carry out their work to a high standard could easily result in a derailment.

So long as any human element remains, however, there may be an occasional accident. Any loss of life is tragic but the Western Region and the Great Western Railway before it can be proud of their record that during the 85 completed years of this century there have been only 17 accidents in which there has been any loss of life among passengers and in this long period only 86 passengers have been killed. Since 1942 there have been only five such accidents.

Comparable statistics for passengers killed in road transport accidents covering the same period and area as the Western figures are not available but when the figure of well over 2,000 persons killed when travelling in vehicles on the roads in this country in 1983 alone is quoted, the comparisons speak for themselves.

Chapter Fourteen

Track and Signalling Development

The earliest type of track, designed by Brunel for the broad gauge, has been described already and it persisted in narrow gauge form into the very early years of this century on lines that had previously been broad gauge. On lines originally laid with the narrow gauge, however, a cross-sleepered track with iron rails had been adopted. Steel rails were first introduced in 1867 and by the early 1880s had become almost universal. While early rails had been of double-head section, and in theory could be turned upside down to extend their life, the later steel rails were of bullhead section with their weight increasing from 86lbs per yard in 1882 to 97½lbs per yard in 1900. Subsequently the Great Western adopted the British Standard 95lbs per yard rail to fall into line with other British companies which adopted it as their standard.

It was after the Second World War that there was a steady changeover to the heavier flat-bottom rail, the weight of which varied over the years from 113lbs per yard to 109lbs per yard and back to 113lbs per yard today. Initially wooden sleepers were used with elastic spike fastenings which in time lost their tension and grip in the sleepers. Later, following extensive experimental work, prestressed concrete sleepers with continuously welded flat-bottom rail were adopted as the standard and much heavier track needed for present day high speeds and heavy axle loads of up to 25 tons. This track uses Pandrol fastenings between rail and sleeper. These have no bolts or screws needing to be tightened periodically and thus require only a minimum of maintenance.

It has often been asked why the old jointed track needs expansion joints whereas the modern continuously welded track does not. The answer lies in the fact that steel, when heated without restraint, expands freely and fills the expansion joint but, if expansion is forcibly prevented, a pressure proportional to the increase in temperature builds up within the rail and unless it is restrained laterally it will buckle and thus release the internal pressure. Continuously welded track is restrained longitudinally by the lack of expansion gaps and restrained laterally by the design of the fastening between rail and sleeper and the stone ballast which surrounds each sleeper. To ensure that the amount of temperature increase is kept within safe limits the rails are adjusted to be free of stress at 80°F. This is done by hydraulically stretching them by a calculated amount equal to the expansion which would occur with a temperature increase to 80°F from that applying at the time of laying in. If the laying in temperature is already above 80°F the adjustment has to be made later in the year when the temperature is lower. The figure of 80°F is selected so that, in addition to avoiding buckling, the tension created in the rails in very cold weather is below that which would cause a fracture or, on curved track, would pull the rails out of alignment.

For crossing work hardwood timber is used to support the steelwork in main lines and it is here that the civil engineering and signal departments are brought closely together in essential co-operation, for the maintenance work of one impinges on the other very closely. In the earliest days of railways this was not necesary since there were few signals and switches were hand-operated. The earliest Great Western signals were of the 'disc and crossbar' type, the disc indicating 'proceed' and the crossbar indicating 'stop'. These were supplemented by fantail caution boards. On the narrow gauge lines north of Wolverhampton semaphore signals were adopted and in the 1860s the Great Western extended their use to the southern part of its territory. Eventually they became universal.

The early signals and points were not interlocked with each other but the need for additional safety measures to prevent conflicting movements of trains became apparent and the first interlocked signal frame was installed in 1860. Their use was extended steadily afterwards so that by 1882 over 80% of signals and points on passenger lines were interlocked mechanically

Disc and crossbar signal at the Didcot Railway Centre and with mixed gauge track in the foreground *Author*

signals and modern multiple aspect colour light signalling, where one box can control many miles of route.

With the introduction of multiple aspect signalling it was soon realised that the flexibility of working which it gave enabled trains to be worked efficiently with much less track and with simplified layouts, which also made permanent way maintenance simpler and cheaper. The Western has taken the fullest advantage of this and reduced considerably the extent of complicated trackwork such as single and double compounds, double junctions, double crossovers and scissors crossovers. For example, the number of double junctions on the whole of the Western Region is now only about fifty and will be reduced still further when the West of England signalling scheme, based on panel boxes at Westbury and Exeter, and a number of other schemes are completed. There is now only one double junction left west of Cardiff on the South Wales main line and only one west of Aller Junction, Newton Abbot on the route to Penzance, for such is the progress that has been made.

One of the expensive items of signalling is the manned control of level crossing gates where either a signalman or crossing keeper is needed. Large numbers of such crossings have been de-manned by the provision of modern types having flashing road traffic lights, and where the extent and speed of road and rail traffic require, also half or full barriers across the road. In the

in the signal boxes.

In the 1930s in the London area, at Bristol and at Cardiff powerful colour light signals had been installed in place of the semaphores, but it was not until after the Second World War that modern multi-aspect colour light signals appeared on the Western. Now they are universal from Paddington to Pembrey, west of Swansea, to Bridgwater via Bristol, to Heyford on the Birmingham line, between Birmingham and Bristol and, when the latest scheme is completed, they will extend from Reading right through to Menheniot, west of Plymouth. This modern signalling is also in use in some areas outside the limits described above, for example at Penzance, Hereford and in the Carmarthen area.

Again, in the early days of railways trains were worked on the 'time interval' principle, it being laid down that no passenger train might follow another train at normal speed until a period of 10 minutes had elapsed, although it could proceed at caution after an interval of 5 minutes. For freight trains the figures were 15 minutes and 8 minutes respectively. These arrangements lasted until the early 1870s when, with the development of the electric telegraph, instruments were devised which altered the working principle from 'time interval' to 'space interval' so that no train could follow another until the first train had passed a specified point or 'block post', which would be several miles away. This principle is still in use today with both semaphore

Typical automatic half barrier level crossing *Author*

Section of the main line at Twyford with continuous welded rail laid on concrete sleepers and suitable for 125 mph running
British Rail

case of half barrier crossings and open crossings which do not have barriers, the traffic lights and half barriers are actuated automatically by the approach of a train.

In the case of open crossings, the train driver is required to reduce speed and be prepared to stop short of the crossing unless a flashing white light at the crossing indicates to him that the road traffic lights are working correctly.

At a few locations where a signal box adjoining the crossing has been retained for operational reasons, the full barriers are controlled from this box, but in other cases where full barriers are needed but a signal box or local control by a crossing keeper is not, such crossings are operated remotely from another location by a signal-man or crossing keeper who has a view of the crossing on a television screen. Having actuated the traffic lights he is able to check that the barriers are lowered and the crossing clear and safe for trains to pass before pressing a button to release the protecting signals.

All these modern crossings have a good safety record but it is preferable to eliminate level crossings altogether if it can be done economically, by either diverting road traffic or providing a bridge. On the 125mph routes this has been largely achieved. Between Paddington and Bristol, for example, only two level crossings of any kind remain. These are both near Didcot and both are operated by one man located at one of the crossings and controlling the other with the aid of television.

Chapter Fifteen

The Future

In concluding this book it would be appropriate to take a brief look into the future – appropriate because the Great Western was a forward-looking company which introduced many innovations and used its excellent publicity department to ensure that they were widely known. This was a product of that independence of mind which we have already seen as a tradition which has been carried on by the Western Region, while at the same time seeing itself as a part of the 'integrated business' which is British Rail.

The process of adjusting the WR infrastructure to the requirements of future traffic patterns, already in hand, will continue in the shape of removing track which is not essential to efficient working. Part of this process involves singling parts of lightly-used double lines, especially in Cornwall and West Wales. This is made possible by the technology which allows the central control of signalling over long distances, and such is the speed of technical progress that the large new panel signal boxes at Westbury and Exeter may well be the last of their type. Future control centres are likely to be much more compact, with the use of visual display units in place of panels and with microchip technology predominating. In the less densely operated areas, radio is likely to be used in signalling.

Although the building of the motorway system has not yet been completed, the disruption to traffic on those already built and now requiring extensive repairs has focussed attention, not only on the dedicated highway we call the railway, but also on the way both modes of transport can complement each other. Bristol Parkway station is a pioneer in the latter sphere, being situated near the junction of the M4 and M5. Further stations of this kind are envisaged at Iver near the M25, at Hinksey south of Oxford and near the M40, and at Sampford Peverell between Taunton and Exeter, near the M5 and intended to serve as the passenger railhead for a large surrounding area of West Somerset and North Devon. All these stations will also serve a population which is no longer tied to town and city centres and prefers to use the car to reach railheads largely free from urban traffic congestion.

The same thought is behind the proposed new station at Gloucester on the avoiding line between Gloucester South and Barnwood junctions. It would allow more trains to stop at Gloucester without the time-consuming reversal presently necessary at Gloucester Central, which would remain as a city centre terminal for local services.

While much of the Western's freight traffic will continue to be trainloads of coal, oil and stone between terminals owned by the producers or purchasers of these products, the success of the fast overnight Speedlink wagonload service using modern long wheelbase wagons will be further exploited in conjunction with private enterprise as owners of terminals for offloading, distribution and storage. In these cases a complete transport package is marketed, with rail transport forming the trunk haul element. Several schemes are already operating successfully at places like Cardiff and Didcot.

As part of the GWR/WR 150th anniversary celebrations some steam excursion trains will run between Bristol and Plymouth during the summer and between Swindon and Gloucester in August, and will no doubt bring back nostalgic memories of the past. But the main line diesel age is one whose relegation to the past has already been the subject of Western Region planning for some time, in the form of replacement by main line electrification. The WR is presently the only Region which does not operate electric trains and, although in the BR overall plan it does not enjoy top priority, electrification is expected to come in the future – probably between Paddington and Oxford to start with, followed by extensions to Birmingham (which would allow through working between Paddington and Manchester, Liverpool and Glasgow) and afterwards to Bristol, South Wales and the West of England.

All such schemes have to meet stringent Government

The changes in the railway freight activity show up clearly in these contrasting scenes of (above) Slough goods yard in the horse and cart era, and (left) the loading of a train of Foster Yeoman modern high capacity wagons   *British Rail*

financial criteria and the Western believes it can do this, but until the electric trains do start running there is much that can and will be done to meet the challenges of our time, with a dynamic management and the conscientious support of the staff as the backbones of success. And so let us recall again those words of Sir Robert Horne in 1935, for as at the centenary, so also on the 150th anniversary of the Great Western Railway, this is an occasion 'to stir the memory and inspire the imagination' as the Western Region prepares for the journey through the years ahead which point the way towards its double century in the service of all those who 'Go Great Western'.

Ancient and modern combine to span the years as (right) an HST bursts from Box Tunnel (*Geoffrey Body*), while (below) an HST interior scene shows the standards of comfort which 150 years of enterprise have produced *British Rail*

GWR 150 Official Souvenir Items

	Price £	Postage £
Brunel statue. Half life-size, painted (Ltd. 12)	975.00	incl.
Brunel statue. 12″ bronze (Ltd. 12)	850.00	incl.
Brunel statue. 12″ bronze resin	145.00	3.00
Glass decanter	19.95	2.50
Matching wine glass	9.95	1.50
Decanter and six wine glasses	75.00	incl.
Commemorative engraved goblet	69.50	incl.
Set of 4 railway letter stamps in presentation pack	2.75	incl.
First souvenir cover for each railway letter stamp (state Iron Duke, City of Truro, 47500, InterCity 125)	2.00	incl.

	Pre 1923	1930–1923	Post 1930	
Standard Table Mats* – Set of six	91.35	75.60	71.66	1.50
Set of four	60.90	50.40	47.77	1.50
Large Table Mats*				
Set of six	107.25	91.50	87.57	1.50
Set of four	71.50	61.00	58.38	1.50
Trays*				
Large	45.50	37.27	34.44	1.50
Standard	40.25	34.16	31.46	1.50

Coasters	Single	Set of 4	Set of 6	
GWR coat of arms	2.50	9.80	14.70	0.75
GW150 logo	0.80	2.62	3.93	0.75
Ruler (state King George V or Firefly)	6.56			0.40

*Each incorporating genuine GWR share certificate.

	Price £	Postage £
Bone China Durham Vase (Ltd. 150)	99.95	2.50
Plate – 22cm – multi-colour	13.95	1.60
Plate – 22cm – chocolate and cream	8.75	1.60
Pentland mug – multi-colour	4.25	1.25
Pentland mug – chocolate and cream	3.50	1.25
Thimble	2.95	0.36
Ladies enamel pill box	45.00	1.50
Glassware		
Firefly paperweight – amber millefiori cane (Ltd. 500)	54.95	2.00
GWR seal paperweight	8.95	1.35
Box Tunnel paperweight	8.95	1.35
Bristol Bowl – Clifton Suspension Bridge	26.95	2.00
Brunel Bowl – Royal Albert Bridge	26.95	2.00
Brunel Tankard	23.50	2.00
Crystal plate – 9″ diameter (state North Star, Lord of the Isles, Firefly, King George V, City of Truro, Hall Class, County Class, Brunel, GWR coat of arms, or GW150 logo)	29.95	2.50
Brass period candle holder/snuffer (state GWR coat of arms or GW150 logo)	27.75	2.50
Dimpled tankard – one pint	3.50	1.50
Dimpled tankard – half pint (state GWR coat of arms or GW150 logo)	2.99	1.00
Engraved Mirror –		
Saltash Bridge – 15″ × 24″	44.95	3.50
Saltash Bridge – 12″ × 15″	37.95	2.75
Engraved Mirror –		
GWR coat of arms – 15″ × 24″	41.25	3.50
GWR coat of arms – 12″ × 15″	34.45	2.75
(state pine or walnut frame)		
GW150 bade – oblong × 1″	0.95	0.20
Key fob	1.30	0.25
Collectors badge – boxed	2.15	0.30
Button badge	0.40	incl.
Brunel lapel badge	1.00	incl.
GWR coat of arms – boxed collectors badge	1.95	0.30
Firefly medal – bronze (Ltd. 2,500)	20.00	incl.
Firefly medal – silver (Ltd. 500)	86.25	incl.
Firefly medal – gold (Ltd. 25)	935.00	incl.
Firefly medal – full set (gold, silver and bronze)	1040.00	incl.
Large framed print (13″ × 16½″)	12.65	1.72
Small framed print (7″ × 9″)	5.75	0.55
Large hessian blockmount (14½″ × 10½″)	8.60	1.10
Small hessian blockmount (6½″ × 8½″)	3.99	0.46
Large blockmount (8″ × 12″)	3.70	0.98
Small blockmount	1.70	0.35
Place mats – set of 6 boxed	10.35	1.72
Coasters – set of 6 boxed	3.10	0.46
Coasters – set of 6 flat packed	2.65	0.46
Clock – wall fitting (state City of Truro or King George V in all cases)	22.00	1.72
The Great Western Railway – 150 Glorious Years	14.95	1.75
The Royal Road – 150 Years of Enterprise	2.95	0.40
Western Handbook – A Digest of GWR & WR Data	2.95	0.40
Combined volume	4.95	0.70
Combine volume – hardback (Ltd.)	7.95	0.98
GWR Magazine – Centenary Number (reprint)	4.95	0.65
Etched Brass Locomotive (Mounted) (state Great Western, The Queen, City of Truro, King George V, Castle Class)	25.50	1.75
Tea Towel/Wall Hanger		
Western Region locomotives	1.95	0.30
Brunel's Architecture	1.95	0.30
Great Western Resource Pack –		
Thames to Severn	5.95	2.00
The West Country	5.95	2.00
South Wales	5.95	2.00
All three versions	14.95	2.50

Orders to AVON-ANGLIA PUBLICATIONS, ANNESLEY HOUSE, 21 SOUTHSIDE, WESTON-SUPER-MARE, AVON BS23 2QU
Prices subject to alteration and items subject to availability. Please allow 28 days for delivery.

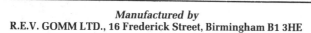

BOOKS ON THE GREAT WESTERN RAILWAY

THE GREAT WESTERN RAILWAY
150 Glorious Years

General Editors:
Patrick Whitehouse and
David St John Thomas

To celebrate the 150th birthday an outstanding team has been brought together to produce this superb large volume. Patrick Whitehouse and David St John Thomas write about the GWR they knew, the locomotives, branch lines, summer Saturday peak traffic and other operations. O. S. Nock, Basil Cooper, Geoffrey Kichenside and others explore their specialities in depth. A remarkable collection of photographs, many previously unpublished, including genuine GWR colour enhance the text and the famous pre-1947 map of the system is included.

8530 5   £14.95

3rd Edition

GREAT WESTERN COACHES: FROM 1890

Michael Harris

The text of the original work published 15 years ago has been revised extensively and updated. A larger page size has allowed better use to be made of the 200 illustrations which will be valuable not only as a record but as an aid to modellers.

8950 8   £16.00

From David & Charles in the Anniversary Year

GWR Quiz

Anthony J Lambert and **Geoffrey Kichenside**

A quiz to challenge the depth and extent of the readers knowledge, 80 prize questions are included – the prize, a footplate trip on a GWR engine at the Severn Valley Railway, plus lunch for two in the restaurant car.

8661 1   £3.95

New Edition

THE GREAT WESTERN RAILWAY
A New History

Frank Booker

The first popular one-volume history of the most loved of all lines, now including colour, reflecting the outlook, social climate and economic trends of the early Victorian age and the first fifty years of this century.

0 946537 16 X   £9.95

TALES OF THE GREAT WESTERN RAILWAY

O S Nock

A unique, fascinating and sometimes humourous account of a major railway and how it ran. O. S. Nock writes on a wide variety of Great Western happenings, in motive power, rolling stock, signalling, civil engineering and much more including personalities.

8050 8   £7.50

GREAT WESTERN LOCOMOTIVE DESIGN
A Critical Appreciation

The Rev John C Gibson

From the turn of the century and for nearly 70 years until the end of steam on BR, Great Western design and practice were at the forefront of locomotive engineering. But what were the locomotives really like in service? Were they the acme of perfection to enginemen and did Great Western fitters have an easier task with component standardisation than those on other lines? John Gibson writes from his own experience and first hand knowledge of others similarly involved, examining the detail of the engines, how they handled, how they behaved in service and what they were like to maintain.

8606 9   £9.95

● **Other GWR books – why not send for our complete catalogue**

BOURNE'S GREAT WESTERN RAILWAY
J C Bourne
4688 1   £65.00

BRUNEL'S BRITAIN
Derrick Beckett
7973 9   £9.95

GREAT WAY WEST:
The History & Romance of the Great Western Route to the West
David St John Thomas
0 946537 15 1   £6.50

GREAT WESTERN ADVENTURE
J B Hollingsworth
8108 3   £6.95

GWR ENGINES, NAMES AND NUMBERS
5367 5   £5.95

GWR STARS, CASTLES & KINGS
(combined Volume)
O S Nock
7977 1   £12.50

New Edition
SUMMER SATURDAYS IN THE WEST
David St John Thomas &
Simon Rocksborough Smith
0 946537 04 6   £6.95

(Locomotive Monograph series)
STANDARD GAUGE GREAT WESTERN 4-4-0s Part 1 1894-1910
O S Nock
7684 5   £6.50

A Regional History of the Railways of Great Britain series

Vol 1 THE WEST COUNTRY
David St John Thomas
8152 0   £10.95

Vol 7 THE WEST MIDLANDS
Rex Christiansen
0 946537 00 3   £10.95

Vol 11 NORTH & MID WALES
Peter Baughan
7850 3   £9.95

Vol 12 SOUTH WALES
D S M Barrie
7970 4   £10.95

Vol 13 THAMES & SEVERN
Rex Christiansen
8004 4   £9.95

To complete our GWR titles in 1985 we expect to re-publish in the Autumn
A HISTORY OF GWR GOODS WAGONS

○ ISBN prefix 0 7153 unless otherwise stated

All books available from **The David & Charles Bookshop, 36 Chiltern Street, London W1M 1PH** (01-486-6959) open Mon-Fri 9.30-5.30 and Sat 10.00-1.00: **Ian Allan Book Centre, 22 Birmingham Shopping Centre, Birmingham**: through all bookshops or direct from **David & Charles Newton Abbot Devon TQ12 4PU.**

DAVID & CHARLES
BRUNEL HOUSE NEWTON ABBOT DEVON

Tel (0626) 67047 24 hour answering service